The Religious Within Experience and Existence

Patrick L. Bourgeois

The Religious Within Experience and Existence

A Phenomenological Investigation

Duquesne University Press
Pittsburgh, Pennsylvania

Copyright © 1990 by Duquesne University Press
Published by Duquesne University Press
600 Forbes Avenue
Pittsburgh, PA 15282

All Rights Reserved

Library of Congress Cataloging in Publication Data

Bourgeois, Patrick L.
The religious within experience and existence:
a phenomenological investigation/Patrick L. Bourgeois
p. cm.
Includes bibliographical references.
ISBN 0–8207–0214–5. — ISBN 0–8207–0215–3 (pbk.)
1. Experience (Religion) 2. Religion. I. Title
BL53. B642 1989   89–38120
291. 4'2'01—dc20   CIP

This book has been composed in
Linotron Palatino

Printed in the United States of America

For
DANNY AND PEGGY
Endless sources of joy

Contents

Acknowledgements   ix

Introduction   1

Chapter One:
    Religious Experience and Philosophy   7

Chapter Two:
    Phenomenology of Religious Experience   34

Chapter Three:
    Existential Dimension of Religious Experience   56

Chapter Four:
    Religious Existence and Existential Phenomenology   81

Chapter Five:
    Finite Religious Existence, Indirect
    Expressions, and Totality   107

Index   129

Acknowledgements

I greatly appreciate the grants from Loyola University making possible the completion of this work.

I would like to express my appreciation to Alvin J. Holloway, S.J., a longtime friend who, as chairman of the philosophy department, has constantly supported research by department members and provided the atmosphere for a department seriously committed to philosophical inquiry. I would also like to thank two special friends who have made philosophy enjoyable and challenging: first, Sandra B. Rosenthal, who, for twenty years, has been a special colleague and unique friend in philosophical inquiry; and to Gary B. Herbert, whose friendship and challenging philosophical differences have been rewarding.

I would like to thank Gladys H. Hallaron for perusing and correcting the text. I owe a debt of gratitude to Susan B. Wadsworth for her many helpful suggestions and for making the text more readable, and to John Dowds for making the publication process palatable.

Introduction

This study focuses upon religious experience in order to derive from it, if possible, elements essential to human experience and existence. As a descriptive account of experience and of existence, such an analysis can be brought to the foundational level grounding all philosophical inquiry and, at the same time, raise the question of the totality within human experience and thinking. Thus it can be seen that, although this study is essentially focused on a specific type of experience, such an inquiry necessarily involves all-pervasive philosophical questioning. The chapters of this study encompass that polarity between the focus on a specific type of human experience and the fundamental and all-pervasive philosophical question of reason's demand for totality.

The first chapter of this study treats the need for philosophical reflection on religious experience and the nature of descriptive philosophical reflection which attempts to initiate its focus in such a way as to grasp religious experience in relation to the whole gamut of human experience. This chapter provides both a clear picture of the type of analysis to be undertaken and states the problem involved in initially focusing on such an object of reflection as religious experience. It further deals with the problem of finding a focus on religious experience which is not biased by personal prejudice, therefore not predetermining the conclusion. In order to find such an initial focus, *conflicting* views of the nature of the object of religious experience will be considered. Hence the opposition between the views of William James and of John Dewey will be dealt with.

Two points in considering James's view of religious experience bring the discussion in this chapter to a point of rapprochement with Dewey's view of the religious qualities of experience, helping us considerably to avoid an unwarranted restriction in our initial focus on the correlation between the lived level of religious experience and its object. First, James's extrication of religious experience from institutional or secondhand religion is similar to Dewey's complete dichotomy between religions and the religious qualities of experience. Second, James and Dewey can be brought together to some extent with regard to what each has to say about the object of religious experience. Thus, by means of some extrapolation between the subject's adjustment and the object of religious experience, an initial focus is set up for the further analysis in the second chapter, which delves into the fundamental structures of such experience. By overcoming the conflicts between James and Dewey, certain elements of a false start are avoided, allowing the analysis of the next chapter to begin with an acceptable basis which is often overlooked.

Chapter Two describes and analyzes the basic dimensions, structures and nature of religious experience by simply invoking a few common cases. In analyzing the instances of various different cases, certain aspects of the person who is undergoing religious experience become clear, as do certain aspects of the object of religious experience. The religious response clearly involves the whole person in such a way as to include the realm of feeling in some practical commitment implicitly including some intellectual content, even if, perhaps, it is only the awareness of projected ideals. Consequently, religious experience is a response involving the total person, even when it is not a total response.

The parallel descriptive analysis of the object of religious experience reveals the object and its claim of ultimacy, but clearly shows the limits of such a claim. In fact, the character of the object of religious experience which emerges is the ultimacy which is equally common to any God claim or to Dewey's projected ideals. Any reflection which attempts to remain descriptive instead of speculative must remain within the limits of that type of reflection which lets the experience speak for itself within the limits of what it can reveal on its own. Ultimacy, or the claim to ultimacy in general, is the essential dimension of the object, with specifications added from within an assumed faith framework. Therefore, although this reflective analysis does not deny or justify any post-option claims, it shows that religious experience is not self-validating. However, this chapter shows religious experience to be constituted by an adjustment involving the whole person, the theoretical, the practical and the affective, in a response to an object which, present within experience, is regarded as having ultimacy or a context of ultimacy.

Chapter Three delves into the fundamental level of lived experience in existence as the root and foundation of religious experience. Consequently, it shows a fundamental openness at the heart of human existence as the foundation of all experience, including religious experience. It becomes clear, however, that on this foundation level, the structures of existence are neutral to God belief or to God nonbelief. Religious belief, practices and interpretations exist within an option, i.e., the option for God belief, in contrast to the option against God belief.

The discussion in this chapter leads into the realm of the existential openness of human being-in-the-world, thereby going one step further than the previous chapter. At this level, the nature of the root of knowledge and being can be discussed without the presupposition of theism or atheism reigning supreme at the outset. Furthermore, the limits of this level, especially in relation to the whole realm of presuppositions with which philosophy begins, can be made thematic, but only in relation to the question of the nature and claims of religious experience.

Further, this takes up the essential line of thinking set forth in the earlier chapters of this book, bringing to the fore the context and the presuppositions which accompany any such reflection, such as the already understood world and the correlation between humans and this world as the context of action, of thought, of reflection, or of religious experience. This foundational level as the point of interaction between humans as enjoying a unique being, and the world as their context of response, to which this whole analysis of religious experience has brought us, deals with the common background for all philosophical reflection as the point from which it emerges and to which it returns.

Thus, the analysis of religious experience in this book has led to the central place of lived experience as leading to an analysis of its existential foundations and of the foundation and origin of philosophical reflection. Throughout the analysis of existence as foundational, the circle involved in understanding is brought to light, so that the implicitly grasped prereflective and prephilosophical dimensions of existence are brought to explicit reflection and clarified in a philosophically explicit manner. What is accepted as the guiding light at the outset of making an *implicit understanding* an *explicit understanding* is seen to take on great importance. For this sets the whole course on its way, showing the importance of the initial stance toward presuppositions. Hence, great importance must be placed on the explication of presuppositions underlying reflection, in the process of which any reflection—such as reflection on religious experience—finds its proper ground.

This chapter, then, explicitly focuses on the relationship between presuppositions and religious experience, including its roots in concrete existence and the existential structure of openness to things, to ourselves, to the world, and to being as such. Although this does not, and indeed, cannot, on this level, be interpreted as *necessarily* a relation to an Absolute Being or even to a Sacred, it can, on a different level of reflection, be interpreted in that way. Therefore, the neutrality on this level can become the base for specific reflections on a different level.

This investigation supports the insight that on the foundational level of existence, there is a neutral structure operative in either the theistic or the atheistic presupposition. No metaphysical claim is made on the presupposed level. The main focal point of this analysis is to liberate the foundational level from the claim of a certain presupposed metaphysical structure which is not justified by an unbiased analysis. Such a presupposed faith is within an option and, as such, has not been sufficiently founded and has been wrongly presupposed, since the existential or foundational ground for either option has not been philosophically established. Consequently, this book attempts to establish a proper ground for all philosophical reflection, and, at once, to lay the foundation for other considerations which might try to justify either option further than can be done on the descriptive level.

Chapter Four pursues further the consequences of the conclusions of the preceding investigations, especially relevant to the neutrality of presuppositional existence. For it is here that the move from religious convictions, retained within a specific option, to a philosophical analysis of human existence often allows a subtle religious presupposition to remain intact. To orient this study of human existence precisely as religious yet neutral to God belief and to the adherence to the Sacred on the ontic level, a brief discussion of contemporary humanism, inclusive of a philosophically acceptable view of the religious in existence, will prove foundational. For such a reflection on a viable contemporary humanism ties together the themes of the preceding investigations, while at the same time laying the foundation for a critique of a view of human existence which pervades the use of phenomenology in theology today, and the treatments of the ontic relation to the Sacred usually central to such use of phenomenology. Thus, the purpose of this chapter is to explicate more adequately the foundational character of human existence within an existential phenomenology as a pervasively contemporary philosophy.

Continuing the direction of Chapter Four, Chapter Five

focuses on the indirect access to totality within a contemporary philosophy that is mindful of the limits of finite human existence in tension with reason's demand for totality. In addition, this chapter attempts to focus on the consequences of such a philosophical limit placed by human reason. Thus, this chapter attempts to bring the previous reflection upon the foundations and eidetic dimensions of religious existence within being-in-the-world to its indirect expression. The fundamental dynamics of such expression within the interrelations of imagination, understanding, intuition and reason reveal both the central role of the imagination and, at once, the foundational character of reason. In developing this indirect access to the totality and consequent to the previous investigations of this study, a subtle critique of a certain view of existence becomes necessary. This final stage of reflection lays bare the ontological foundation for the religious option and indirect expressions in the openness of the human being (Dasein), and, further, it orients reflection emerging from and required by the foundational explications of this entire study.

This book does not attempt to have the last word but, rather, only the first word. This first level of consideration, as preliminary and fundamental, is far more limited than many philosophers and philosopher-theologians today want to admit. Yet it is richer than most have allowed it to be.

CHAPTER ONE

Religious Experience and Philosophy

When the U.S. space lab plummetted to earth some years ago, a naive and superstitious group attributed it to a manifestation of evil, a god angered, or something of that nature. Such a belief arouses amusement and mirth in sophisticated people. When the context is changed from such an event to questions of the nature of religious experience and mysticism or to the question of the existence of God, many apparently sophisticated people react in a similar way. For it is often said that we today are too intelligent and educated for such naive and primitive beliefs, and that we have outgrown the God of childhood.

This reaction not only raises serious questions for anyone interested in the religious realm, but also, at once, raises questions of a strictly philosophical nature. One of the chief difficulties in delving into such inquiries springs from the fact that thinkers usually begin their reflections on religious matters from within an already made commitment, which influences the progress of their investigation even though it has not been critically analyzed and understood.[1] For example, people who read Dewey tend to respond strongly in favor of or in opposition to his atheism, depending on their own mind-set. This difficulty is not easily overcome even by the serious philosopher intensely trying to prevent such presuppositional attitudes and allegiances from being operative in his reflection.[2]

---

1. This influence from an already made commitment within the context of presuppositions will be studied in later chapters, especially in Chapter Four. Further, certain aspects of it will emerge in the later part of this chapter in reflecting on William James's view of the roots of faith and the nature of religious experience.

2. As shall be seen, the structure and development of Chapter Two is

The ensuing investigations will attempt to explicate in a descriptive philosophy the presuppositional base from which philosophical reflection on religious experience and religious existence—and indeed, by extension, all reflection—proceed. More specifically, this study attempts to show the philosophical substrate for phenomenological theology by employing a phenomenology of religious experience to explicate the openness and transcendence of existence, thus radicalizing phenomenology in theology, yet also imposing serious limits on this descriptive level of method. Nevertheless, even within this deliberately limited focus, the analysis illuminates the nature of human experience, of knowledge emerging within experience, and of reality known. Indeed, as fundamental and preliminary, this analysis sheds light upon any further investigation of religion and of God, for a basic level of human existence will be seen to ground both theistic and atheistic responses to the questions about God's existence and about the experience of God. More importantly, the discussion will attempt to show the limitation of such a philosophical and fundamental analysis. It is to the discussion of the need for a philosophical mode and method of analysis that we must briefly turn.

THE NEED FOR THIS PHILOSOPHICAL REFLECTION

The need for philosophical and philosophical-theological reflection is not always admitted by religious enthusiasts. Some instances of fanaticism in recent public memory call

---

deliberately staged in order to avoid certain prejudices in approaching the questions central to this enquiry. Some of the philosopher-theologians obliquely referred to include: Langdon Gilkey, in *Naming the Whirlwind: The Renewal of God Language* (New York: The Bobbs-Merril Co., 1969); David Tracy, especially in *Blessed Rage for Order: The New Pluralism* (New York, The Seabury Press, 1975); and Edward Farley, in *Ecclesial man: A Social Phenomenology of Faith and Reality* (Philadelphia: Fortress Press, 1975).

for such a reflection, although even these cases will not convince antagonists who are opposed for "religious reasons" to such a reflection.

The religious fanaticism of Jim Jones and the Jonestown sect and of the Ayatollah Khomeini and his ardent followers have disturbed even religious people, although they usually cannot stipulate precisely what troubles them about these cases. To go beyond a certain gut level rejection of the extremes in these cases requires serious reflection on balance and extremes in religious commitments. Among the many types of possible reflection, the philosophical is the most far-reaching and critical. As shall be seen, it is presupposed and demanded by the enlightening analyses of such disciplines as those of psychology and sociology. In showing the advantages of such a philosophical analysis, the discussion must make clear the precise uniqueness proper to philosophical reflection of this kind.

The attempt to unravel the precise difference between the philosophical and nonphilosophical questioning about the nature of religious experience is best initiated by focusing upon psychological accounts, religious testimony or theological reflection as instances of nonphilosophical treatments. Psychological treatment, for instance, of religious experience or of other types of experience is not, as such, a philosophical reflection. Yet such treatments can be accurate and true. No matter how psychologically astute a treatment might be, it is not, as such, any more philosophical than a profound, sincere and true testimony of a religious experience. This second instance of the presentation of religious experience, a testimony or witness, emerges from within a religious commitment and, as such, is certainly not philosophical. Further, the strictly theological and religious reflection on religious experience, as such, is not philosophical. This will become apparent in the ensuing discussion.

Such nonphilosophical instances of presenting religious experience mentioned above acutely raise the question of the specific difference between philosophical reflection and nonphilosophical reflection. That difference is intrinsic to philosophical reflection upon any experience or any aspect of reality. Consequently, even though this treatment is specific in focusing upon the reflection on religious experience, the overall importance of the basic question of philosophical reflection cannot be exaggerated.[3]

Both the point of view and the object of philosophical reflection differentiate it from other modes of reflection. The uniqueness of its point of view involves an ultimacy[4] which makes it basic and all-pervasive, i.e., sets it apart as a uniquely different mode of inquiry because anything it focuses on is considered from a point of view which is uniquely ultimate. For instance, both psychology and sociology consider human behavior from different points of view within the limits of two differing particular sciences. Philosophy, however, has a certain unique quality in focusing on human behavior because it considers human behavior not from the point of view of sociology (*socios*) or of psychology (*psyche*), but basically from the point of view of its relation to all actual and possible behavior, or to reality as such, or to all human behavior in relation to cognition and values as such. Thus, the cognitive structures and the realities which they make accessible are the ultimate concern of philosophical enquiry which focuses upon such objects of reflection as behavior. The same

---

3. It must be kept clearly in mind that this is merely a brief account of philosophy in general, as preliminary to delving into phenomenology as the contemporary philosophy and method to be employed in this study. Yet it must be emphasized that this is not a work on method, and thus, a lengthy treatment on the nature of philosophy as such or on phenomenology as method is not necessary.

4. The use of the word "ultimacy" must not be misunderstood in this context or in later context in this study. It does not refer to an absolute being or substance. Rather, it means the end of a process, or the most far-reaching, the all-pervasive or all-inclusive, or final point. This use of "ultimate" will become clear in the following paragraphs on the uniqueness of philosophy in distinction from certain specific sciences, and it will be employed later in this study in the treatment of the object of religious experience.

holds true, however, for philosophical reflection on religious experience.

Therefore, philosophical reflection on religious experience can be seen to differ essentially from psychological or sociological reflection on religious experience.[5] Whereas such psychological and sociological reflections have specific points of view, philosophical reflection is a basically all-pervasive and ultimate point of view, in that it investigates the structure and implications of the epistemic dimension of the religious, and, at the same time, the reality to which these structures give access. The mode of reflection attempts to understand or explain religious experience in an adequately rational way. This philosophical dimension of reflection must be further explored, especially in its focus on religious experience.

A philosophical understanding as such must be distinguished from mythic[6] and dogmatic accounts. The philosophical understanding, based on rational evidence and insight, differs from a religious mythic account in that the latter has recourse to a story which is presented and accepted from within a religious belief and tradition, or which is adhered to superstitiously. Similarly, a dogmatic presentation of religious experience, unlike a philosophical approach, presents something—for example, an interpretation of religious experience—demanding belief in the presentation for reasons other than evidence which ap-

---

5. These remarks are not meant to belittle in any way the contemporary scientific and sociological studies of religion. It simply aims to supplement these studies with a necessary philosophical reflection.

6. These brief remarks on myth point out simply that philosophy as such is not mythic. It is not meant to exclude myth from the interest and relevance of philosophy. Many writers today in philosophy and philosophical theology incorporate a philosophy of myth, metaphor and poetic language into their strictly philosophical accounts. For the centrality of myth, symbol and metaphor, see Paul Ricoeur: e.g., *The Symbolism of Evil* trans. by Emerson Buchanan (New York, Evanston and London: Harper & Row, 1967); Other authors who find it necessary to treat seriously the role of myth, symbol and metaphor, to name only a few, are David Tracy, Langdon Gilkey, Edward Farley and Hans-Georg Gadamer.

11

peals to reason, as, for instance, an appeal to authority.

The philosophical understanding, distinguished above from mythic and dogmatic accounts, must be clarified in relation to religious options. Such a reflection, as philosophical, must not spring unawares from within a specific option. For the most part, these reflections are undertaken by committed theists from within the acceptance of their religious tradition and its beliefs, dogmas, rituals, mores, etc. But a philosophical reflection should include an ever-increasing awareness of what such a prior commitment entails, and should, as far as possible, prescind in some way from the condition of the option or prior commitment.[7] This becomes clear if a contrast is made between theistic and atheistic reflection. If either the atheist or the theist reflect on religious experience from within either of these specific options, the network of presuppositions influences the philosophical reflection in a way which is philosophically naive and prejudicial unless adverted to and explicated adequately. Consequently, it is clear that philosophical reflection on religious experience cannot demand that an option not be made, but rather that the option be admitted, focused upon and explicated. As a matter of fact, we cannot fail to have certain options, nor to operate within them. Nevertheless, such philosophical reflection must become explicitly aware of the network of presuppositions of a particular problem, and, working through and not around them, attempt to do justice to the particular option. The present discussion can turn now to the object of philosophical reflection, which is the second

---

7. In the present analysis, the "prescinding" means the reduction used as a technique of phenomenological method. Such a reduction does not cut off what is bracketed or focused upon within reflection. Rather, it simply achieves a change or a shift in focus. The reduction as an element of phenomenological method will be treated later in this chapter. It will be seen that the controversies over the role, nature, and status of the reduction are far-reaching and significant. The appropriation of phenomenology as method for the present study, however, includes a rather simple use of the reduction as a technique of method.

specifying difference between philosophy and other modes of reflection.

The object of philosophical reflection, just as its point of view, has a uniqueness which sets this reflection apart from other modes of reflection. This object, regardless of any specific focus, includes at least implicitly the dimension of ultimate constitution of reality. Likewise, this dimension of ultimacy includes at least implicitly the further character of the totality of all that is. Thus, when the object of philosophical reflection is specific, focusing, for instance, on humans or on religious experience instead of focusing directly and immediately on being, reality or existence, the specifying difference of the ultimate constitution of reality is still the pervasive and at least implicit concern. The relevance and application of this to philosophical reflection on religious experience is easily clarified.

Philosophical reflection, focusing specifically on the nature, structure, meaning and implications of religious experience, as the object of reflection, does not uproot this experience from human experience in general. Consequently, religious experience is grasped in relation to all other human experiences as such, and in relation to its own existential dimensions. The present analysis of religious experience cannot be characterized simply as philosophical without qualification. After setting up the problem for a more general philosophical reflection, a specific focus and method of analysis will take over and unfurl ever deeper dimensions of religious experience. Thus, phenomenology is the specific method for this philosophical analysis. Certain general aspects of this phenomenological procedure should be made explicit, but without losing sight of that which is to be analyzed.

The basic theme of phenomenology, "to the thing itself," directs an analysis to focus specifically on what is being analyzed without accepting prior commitments, presuppositions or judgments. Although at first glance this seems to state a truism, it undercuts whole traditions and systems of philosophy, directing reflection to a fundamental consideration which is usually overlooked.[8] "To the thing itself," for instance, directs the analysis to focus on religious experience as it is lived through, instead of allowing a previously accepted definition or an already set characterization of religious experience to distort what the analysis focuses on and is able to see. Further, such false approaches begin with the acceptance of an already presupposed framework, characterization and understanding of what is to be understood. A phenomenological approach, as philosophical, attempts to undercut these various presupposed understandings without necessarily condemning them as wrong. Further, it attempts reflectively to undercut them in order to get to the "thing itself" in the present analysis, the phenomenon of religious experience on the basic level, which actually is the source of those other presupposed and derived levels of understanding.

To initiate a phenomenological focus on religious experience, at once adequately undercutting presupposed ways of reading such a phenomenon, and achieving a grasp of the experience as the thing itself, involves a specific change of focus usually called phenomenological reduction.[9] In a

---

8. It often happens that aspects of method lead to philosophical positions, especially in the kind of scientism and psychologism rejected by phenomenology. Husserl and later phenomenologists have rejected certain philosophical views as well as claims of the method from which those views spring. Phenomenology has evolved as a method more adequate for dealing with the full gamut of human experience than other methods. The method evolved from the exigency of accounting for the correlation between the objectivity grapsed by consciousness and the lived experiences giving rise to and making possible the objectivity in consciousness. Husserl first focused on the level of logical and mathematical meanings, and over the years gradually deepened his focus to include all realms and levels within the overall field of meanings. Thus for Husserl, the correlation between method and content arises from his constant concern to find the foundations first for mathematics and logic and finally for the whole of the knowing enterprise, leading to the development of a phenomenology of experience.

9. This treatment of the reduction in phenomenology suffices to deal

sense, the term phenomenological reduction is a further specification of the more general theme "to the thing itself." This element of phenomenology is a change or shift of focus which captures and holds the phenomenon, religious experience, as it is lived through, rather than taking it in the sense mentioned above, as the product of a "higher" level of activity, abstract or distorted. As such, this change of focus allows an analysis to grip whatever phenomenon is focused on and to grasp its essential features as it is directly reflected upon.

The theme of phenomenology, "to the thing itself," and the change in focus make possible the grasp of the essential kernel as the necessary element or elements of an experience or of any phenomenon.[10] The essential ele-

---

adequately with the change of focus in general discussed in the text. But, it must be admitted, the controversies over the rule, nature and status of the reduction are far-reaching and significant. See the following: Richard M. Zaner, *The Way of Phenomenology* (New York: Pegasus, 1970), pp. 193–194; Richard H. Holmes, "Is Husserl Committed to Idealism?" *The Monist*, vol. 59, No. 1, 1975: *Husserl: An Analysis of His Phenomenology*, ed. and trans. by Edward G. Ballard and Lester E. Embree, (Evanston: Northwestern University Press, 1967); Edmund Husserl, "Phenomenology," in *Encyclopedia Britannica*, Collier Books (1962). Also, see Patrick L. Bourgeois, "Phenomenology and the Fundamental Structure of Experience," *Philosophy Today*, Summer 1985, pp. 135–141; Patrick L. Bourgeois and Sandra B. Rosenthal, *Thematic Studies in Phenomenology and Pragmatism*, (Holland: Gurner, 1983); and Sandra B. Rosenthal and Patrick L. Bourgeois, *Pragmatism and Phenomenology: A Philosophic Encounter*, (Holland: Gruner, 1980).

10. Husserl distinguishes a whole network of reductions which often are treated in such a way as to enslave the treatment to the theory of reductions instead of allowing the reduction to initiate a change of focus in order to begin phenomenological analysis. The expression used in the text, "the essential kernel" or the necessary "element" actually bespeaks a further restriction of the initial change of focus usually called the eidetic reduction. In Husserl's context, the initial methodological change of focus, the technique of reductions, yields a pure phenomenon, prescinding from consideration of existence and reality and thus overcoming the psychologism of Brentano. The structural eidetic aspect of the pure phenomenon, grasped within an experience, can be derived by the use of phenomenological descriptive method yielding pure experience. For our purposes, all that is meant is that the essential features of the experience, that without which it would not be considered this kind of experience, are to be derived.

ments, for instance, of religious experience are those which are necessary for it to be what it is; or, they are those without which the thing would not be what it is. A certain comparison, then, is involved in this analysis which attempts basically to describe the essential features even by means of showing that, if one is absent, the phenomenon is essentially and radically changed. Such an imaginative variation[11] allows the analysis to get hold of the phenomenon in an adequate description revealing its essential features.

REMARKS CONCERNING PROBLEMS

Two further remarks concerning the nature and the method of this inquiry are necessary before turning to analyze the problem. First, disagreements about the nature and status of this kind of experience and its object should not militate against a fruitful growth in understanding. The method, analysis and procedure of this study do not require or presuppose the acceptance of an initial commitment of faith in a God, faith arising from a particular tradition, or a faith contrary to these.[12] These investigations simply open a vista for anyone interested in understanding the full gamut of human experiences, and hopefully reveal something that is based on the evidence

---

11. Such an "imaginative variation," a technique in the phenomenological method employed within the reductions, involves the role of imagination in varying the phenomenon in free fancy so that its essential features or aspects emerge into clarity. As the imagination varies the phenomenon imaginatively to the point at which it ceases essentially to be what it is, these nonessential elements becomes clear at the same time as the essential elements are seen as essential.

12. It is worth repeating that the methodological technique of reductions employed in phenomenology does not involve cutting off, or rendering inoperative, intentional relations. The reductions simply involve a change of focus and a refocus. In the context of phenomenology of religious experience and faith commitment, faith is not bracketed in the sense of cut off, but rather, while still operative, it is looked upon reflectively in a different focus.

of experience itself. Thus, great care in setting up the problem avoids prejudicing the outcome of the analysis. Precisely this difficulty, avoiding prejudicing the outcome, is the vital concern of a second preliminary remark.

The relation between the object of religious experience and the method of approach, phenomenology, must not be allowed to prejudice the outcome of the analysis by predetermining certain dimensions of the object. Sometimes the appropriation of method is allowed to involve or to include a point of view which necessarily sees the object in a certain way. For instance, mathematical physical science looks from a particular point of view at its objects, thereby predetermining what is seen as aspects of its objects. This is the case in the scientist's focus on quantity within the abstraction of scientific objects from lived experience. The points of view of B.F. Skinner in his behaviorism, or of Masters and Johnson in their studies of sexual behavior, strictly as limited points of view of certain kinds of psychology, reflect similar limiting points of view at the outset of their respective analyses. For Skinner, the limit involves a certain way of seeing behavior according to preaccepted presuppositions or limitations of point of view, for example, in favor of observable and measurable behavior. The same must be said of the research of Masters and Johnson with regard to human sexual behavior: the limitation to physiology of their accounts of sexual behavior and response is a deliberately set limitation of their point of view. However, in the present philosophical analysis of religious experience, a similar limitation cannot be allowed or the fundamental level of experience is lost, and the return to the actual lived-through experience is falsified in favor of something else which is allowed to enter from outside the experience, in terms of which it is explained. To overcome the aforementioned difficulty, then, this analysis must focus on the experience as lived, instead of reading into it the products of any particular points of view. Further, this analysis cannot begin by demanding that the outcome meet prior expectations.

A careful appropriation of a method such as phenomenology does not, however, allow an analysis to avoid presuppositions. Yet such a study is not arbitrary and capricious. The reduction, as the change of focus, and the return "to the thing itself" in experience, permit the presuppositions to remain intact, allowing the structures and meaning of an experience to be grasped in its context or situation. It is with the explicit awareness of the totality of presuppositions that the analysis begins, proceeds and reaches its goal, instead of overlooking or avoiding them.

SETTING UP THE PROBLEM: RELIGIOUS EXPERIENCE

Since some thinkers deny the very meaning of religious experience and its object, or deny the existence of its object and the meaningfulness of this experience itself, these denials should be faced directly before even attempting to throw into focus religious experience as an object for analysis. Thus a paradoxical situation emerges. There is a necessity to know what is to be focused on before beginning the analysis; yet, that is precisely what the analysis is to find out as its outcome and conclusion. The problem can be faced only by careful admission of what is to be done, which in turn is dictated by the problem itself. Instead of beginning by an arbitrary choice of religious experience, the analysis will focus on the tension between the contradictory interpretations of religious experience by William James and John Dewey. Although this involves a postponement of actual phenomenological analysis, such an approach allows the concrete presuppositional context to be more explicitly brought forth as the backdrop for the ensuing analysis, and, at once, further addresses vital questions concerning the whole issue, especially theoretical questions about God belief, God talk, God experience, metaphysical ultimates, etc. The discussion will now turn to the treatments by James and Dewey of religious experience in order to set the stage for a phenomenology of religious experience.

Religious Experience: James and Dewey

The aim at this point is to find a philosophically viable and acceptable descriptive access to religious experience. More specifically, it is to set up a phenomenological focus on this kind of experience by laboring first to find a way to begin which avoids a premature acceptance of presuppositions and assumptions. In order to find an initial focus,[13] cognizant of cultural and situational presuppositions and of personal experience and bias, conflicting views of the nature and object of religious experience will be considered. It will be helpful, therefore, to address the opposition between the views of James and Dewey.

James: Religion Subjectively Considered

James clarifies his concern with religion in the following text, in which he shows a leaning toward the subjective and experiential aspect of religion.

> Religion, therefore, as I now ask you arbitrarily to take it, shall mean for us the *feelings, acts, and experiences of individual men in their solitude, so far as they apprehend themselves to stand in relation to whatever they may consider the divine.* Since the relation may be either moral, physical, or ritual, it is evident that out of religion in the sense in which we take it, theologies, philosophies and ecclesiastical organization may

13. At the end of his two volume history of the phenomenological movement, Herbert Spiegelberg indicates the difficulty in finding the first focus on an object to be considered by means of phenomenology as method. He has appended to his two volume history a lengthy treatment of phenomenological method. It must be mentioned, however, that this is only one appropriation of the method. He has attempted to integrate the salient features of the method, including the difficulty of the initial focus. See Herbert Spiegelberg, *The Phenomenological Movement: A Historical Introduction* (The Hague: Martinus Nijhoff, 1965), vol. II, pp. 653–701.

secondarily grow. In these lectures, however, as I have already said, the immediate personal experiences will amply fill our time, and we shall hardly consider theology or ecclesiasticism at all.[14]

Several points must be understood from the above text in order to properly incorporate James's position into our treatment. First, James admits his rather arbitrary way of looking at religion. It is precisely the flexibility allowed by the arbitrariness which makes it possible for an analysis of religious experience, though not at all close to a focus on religion, to start with James's reflection on religion, since, for him, religious experience is what he actually discusses. James admits that he hopes to "escape much controversial matter by this arbitrary definition of our field."[15]

Further, he explicitly admits the arbitrariness of his view of religion in another text: "and, although it would indeed be foolish to set up an abstract definition of religion's essence, and then proceed to defend that definition against all comers, yet this need not prevent me from taking my own narrow view of what religion shall consist in *for the purpose of these lectures*, or, out of the many meanings of the word, from choosing the one meaning in which I wish to interest you particularly, and proclaiming arbitrarily that when I say 'religion' I mean *that*."[16]

The importance of the second remark is that James, in this above characterization of religion, simply restricts his focus to firsthand religion.[17] His explicit interest is to make a "search rather for the original experiences which were the pattern-setters to all this mass of suggested feeling and imitated conduct."[18] James is therefore clearly interested in this firsthand religion, or, in other words, personal reli-

---

14. William James, *The Varieties of Religious Experience* (New York: Collier Books, 1961), p. 42.
15. James, pp. 42–43.
16. James, p. 40.
17. James, pp. 24, 42.
18. James, pp. 24–25.

gion, characterizing it as "direct personal communion with the divine"[19] and distinguishing it from institutional religion.

James further distinguishes the personal or firsthand religion from the institutional or secondhand religion in the following passage:

> In one sense at least the personal religion will prove itself more fundamental than either theology or ecclesiasticism. Churches, when once established, live at secondhand upon tradition; but the *founders* of every church owed their power of originality to the fact of their direct personal communion with the divine. Not only the superhuman founders, the Christ, the Buddha, Mahomet, but all the originators of Christian sects have been in this case;—so personal religion should still seem the primordial thing, even to those who continued to esteem it incomplete.[20]

James, in limiting the living of the churches to second-hand religion, tends to exclude religious experience from the churches, as John Dewey explicitly does in excluding the religious qualities of experience from religion. In speaking of the person who belongs to established religions, James observes: "His religion has been made for him by others, communicated to him by tradition, determined to fixed forms by imitation and retained by habit."[21] And it is to this that he condemns the religions of those who belong to the churches, reserving for their founders or the originators of sects the "direct personal communion with the divine,"[22] as "original experiences which were the pattern-setters" for secondhand religious life.[23]

In thus extricating religious experience or firsthand religion from the institutions and from secondhand religion, James's view, as shall be seen, has a common element with

---

19. James, p. 42.
20. James, p. 42.
21. James, p. 24.
22. James, p. 42.
23. James, pp. 24–25.

Dewey's complete dichotomy between religious qualities of experience and religions.[24] Although James's main intention is simply to restrict his focus to religious experience and not to consider institutional religion, he cannot totally justify such a complete dichotomy between religion and religious experience, in spite of the fact that there is some basis for his remarks.[25] For even if it is the case that religions tend to institutionalize religious experience, it is prejudicial to say at the outset that this *necessarily* happens,[26] that it is *always* so, and to undercut the possibility of religious experience within religions. It is unfair to assume that religious experience is essentially alien to religions or to place an essential incongruity between them. Even if what that assumption holds is an essential possibility, its place is at the end of an analysis as a result of serious reflection, and not as an assumption implicit in the initial focus of turning to the object to be investigated. Consequently, this phenomenology of religious experience will not allow that dichotomy between religious experience and religion to be considered an essential structure unless this is warranted by further analysis of religious experience as the object of our focus.

James: Religious Experience and Its Object

James's treatment of the object of religious experience can be helpful in preventing distortion of religious experience in our analysis, as well as in leading to further insights with regard to Dewey's view of religious experience. However, it must be emphasized that this study of James's and Dewey's treatments of religious experience is

---

24. This remark is not meant to reduce James's position to that of Dewey, but, rather, to indicate affinities where complete opposition seems at first the only possible relation between James and Dewey. This point will be developed further throughout this chapter.

25. James is seen here not to go as far as Dewey in his account of the dichotomy between religion and religious experience, or, in other words, between first and secondhand religion.

undertaken primarily as an aid to a fundamental phenomenological reflection attempting to obtain an initial grasp of religious experience as it is lived. A consideration of James's view of religious experience and its object will further that endeavor.

James, at least initially in his consideration, does not interpret the object of religious experience explicitly as a supernatural Being, but, rather, seems to leave room for a certain indeterminacy, even though, afterward, he explicitly interprets it as a supernatural Being. This initial ambiguity or neutrality, together with Dewey's treatment, allows an initial focus on religious experience as the object of our reflection, in such a way as to avoid interpreting a certain aspect of religious experience to be essential to it. The following discussion on the object of religious experience should make this point clear.

James's initial statement about the object of religious experience allows for a certain ambiguity, at least if it is taken out of the context of his further explicit reflections. He says: "The divine shall mean for us only such a primal reality as the individual feels impelled to respond to solemnly and gravely and neither by a curse nor a jest."[27] The "divine" in this statement does not necessarily mean a supernatural Being. Nor do the attitude and its characteristics necessitate such a supernatural Being, even though, he says, "There must be something solemn, serious, and tender about any attitude which we denominate religious."[28]

Since James's development goes in a direction other than that of this reflection, two remarks are necessary in order to show how his view actually can further the develop-

---

26. It is precisely the task of this phenomenological investigation, as phenomenological, to ferret out the essential aspects of religious experience, but without allowing any essential dimensions to be assumed at the outset. Thus, the focus, the point of view, and the implicitly grasped thing to be analyzed can be seen to be of vital importance in the setting up of such an analysis.

27. James, p. 48.

28. James, p. 48.

ment of this reflection, and, at the same time, in order to show how he goes in a different direction. The first remark arises from James's lectures themselves where he speaks about the essence of religious experience, which, it must be recalled, is what the present philosophical reflection on religious experience is attempting to derive. James expresses his concern as follows: "The essence of religious experience, the thing by which we finally must judge them, must be that element or quality in them which we can meet nowhere else."[29] James is not at odds, therefore, with the basic thrust of the present inquiry in its attempt to derive the essential and necessary dimensions of religious experience. However, as shall be seen in the next chapter, the philosophical approach employed in the present study can attain the essential kernel of religious experience without giving the prominance to "one-sided, exaggerated and intense" cases as James does.[30] What is essential to such experience must be present in any instance of religious experience, even those which are not intense, one-sided or exaggerated. Nevertheless, James's stress on these "one-sided, exaggerated and intense" cases is certainly not unwarranted. Further, it serves the phenomenological method of our philosophical reflection well, in that his choices bring to the fore cases which, although extreme, are still cases of religious experience, and consequently contain everything essential to religious experience, even though, in some sense, they manifest certain distortions. We can thereby see the use of imaginative variation as an element of method mentioned previously. In James's variety of cases, each, in spite of vast differences, allows this reflection to delve into the common features, especially those aspects constituting the very nature, structure or essence of religious experience. However, as will be seen in Chapter Two, the choice of cases for further develop-

---

29. James, pp. 52–53.
30. James, p. 53.

ment in this analysis will differ vastly from that of James, yet the present analysis will be attuned to his cases as directing the analysis toward the essential dimensions of religious experience.

The second remark distinguishes James's development of the religious hypothesis in other of his works and toward the end of *The Varieties of Religious Experience* from the direction of the present reflection. Although in further chapters of this study certain metaphysical questions in relation to religious experience will emerge, to raise explicitly metaphysical questions in the present context would require leaving the initial phenomenological focus on religious experience so far undertaken, and demand a reflection of an entirely different nature. However, a brief consideration of James's statement of the move from religious experience to a good hypothesis about reality helps to clarify further the nature of the focus being staged throughout James's and Dewey's treatments of religious experience.

> Only when this further step of faith concerning God is taken, and remote objective consequences are predicated, does religion, as it seems to me, get wholly free from the first immediate subjective experience, and bring a real hypothesis into play. A good hypothesis in science must have other properties than those of the phenomenon it is immediately invoked to explain, otherwise it is not prolific enough. God, meaning only what enters into the religious man's experience of union, falls short of being an hypothesis of this more useful order. He needs to enter into wider cosmic relations in order to justify the subject's absolute confidence and place.[31]

It should be clear from this statement that the present analysis, focusing precisely on religious experience as lived through, remains on the level of what James calls "first immediate subjective experience" prior to the move to a "real hypothesis." Thus, the thrust of this analysis aims to

31. James, p. 400.

focus on the experience, analyze it, and derive its structure, rather than move away from it to form an explanatory hypothesis. Nevertheless, the philosophic approach which attempts to explain religious experience and its object in a way which is more speculative, or, in other words, removed from the immediacy of experience, will be discussed later in the present study to show precisely the necessity and importance of such an enterprise to complement the philosophical approach chosen here, and in order to overcome its limitations. The philosophical analysis undertaken here deliberately avoids such far-reaching questions at the outset only to return to them later, in order to make that return better and more solid by supplying it with the best possible foundations—the adequate fundamental analysis of the lived experience of religious experience, presupposed as the ground and limit of all further analysis, even those of a more speculative nature referred to here by James with the notion of hypothesis.

One point concerning James's object of religious experience needs further clarification before turning explicitly to a contrast between the views of James and Dewey on religious experience. It was noted above that James's initial characterization of religion, in its subjective view, could be interpreted to be neutral to a specific object, leaving the object of religious experience simply to be a "primal reality." However, his explicit intention becomes clear in his third lecture of *The Varieties of Religious Experience*, if not before, when he speaks about the reality of the unseen, the primal reality, as unambiguously and clearly supernatural in character. He has spoken early in *The Varieties of Religious Experience* of this "belief that there is an unseen order, and that our supreme good lies in harmoniously adjusting ourselves thereto."[32] As shall be seen in the study of Dewey, James has gone further than necessary in naming the object an unseen order but has correlated it with a

---

32. James, p. 59.

belief and with an adjustment which can be compared and contrasted with that of Dewey. James speaks of this belief and this adjustment as the religious attitude in the soul. "This belief and this adjustment are the religious attitude in the soul."[33] Although the object of this attitude, as the belief and adjustment of response, is vastly different from what Dewey considers to be the object of religious experience, James's view of religious experience lends itself to an interrelation with that of Dewey. And precisely such a treatment serves the purpose of this chapter setting the stage for a basic philosophic analysis of religious experience uncommitted by prior prejudice to a theistic or a nontheistic position, yet, paradoxically, doing justice to religious experience. To further this project and its intention, the discussion must turn briefly to Dewey's treatment of the religious in experience.

Dewey: Religious Experience

THE RELIGIOUS QUALITIES OF EXPERIENCE

Dewey, in spite of his explicitly professed atheistic naturalism, can be of assistance in presenting a focus upon religious experience free from unfounded claims. For in separating and freeing the religious qualities or aspects of experience from religion, he has stripped religious experience down to certain essential aspects. Therefore, the question of the object of religious experience as a primal reality, proposed and developed above in the context of James's *Varieties of Religious Experience*, can be similarly proposed in Dewey's context: i.e., a context which deals with whether the object of religious experience must be a supernatural God. Put another way, the question is whether or not there is such a correlation between the object as God and the religious experience, such that

---

33. James, p. 59.

without God as its object, an experience would not be considered religious.

Although James has been seen to exclude explicitly Dewey's interpretation of the object of religious experience, he at least leaves open the possibility in the ambiguity of some of his earlier formulations. Dewey, however, goes far beyond that point of difference by explicitly and emphatically extricating the religious qualities of experience from religion and religions, holding ultimately the impossibility of religious experience within religions. Yet he intends emphatically to preserve the religious qualities of experience within his atheistic naturalism. He thus disagrees with theists and atheists alike who, from their respective positions, agree about a necessary correlation between religion and the supernatural.

That apparent agreement between atheists and theists about the necessary correlation between religion and the supernatural contains aspects which must be clarified: first, that the supernatural is the necessary object of religious experience; second, that the denial of the reality of the supernatural is, at once, a denial and exclusion of anything religious. For to identify everything religious with the supernatural would mean that the denial of the supernatural excludes the possibility of religion. By contrast, Dewey defines an atheistic alternative which contains some viable dimension of the religious aspect of experience.

In taking such a position, Dewey raises questions which are important for initiating the focus on religious experience within this study. This study's focus should avoid the prejudices highlighted by Dewey, leaving open at the outset the possibility for his interpretation of the religious aspect of experience, even though it does not spring from a God belief, but instead, from the naturalistic belief. While this openness of Dewey's view of religious experience in relation to James's view is helpful in beginning such an unprejudiced analysis, the above comparison and contrast still leaves open the central question of the nature and uniqueness of religious experience. The discussion will now turn to a further treatment of Dewey's analysis of religious experience, as a preparation for Chapter Two, where the essential nature of religious experience will be taken up explicitly.

In extricating the religious aspects of experience from religion, Dewey gets rid of the "excess baggage," that which is not essential to the basic experience. He, rather, considers the basic attitude of adjustment not to be necessarily correlated with any specific object. "It denotes attitudes that may be taken toward every object and every proposed end or idea."[34] He certainly does not wish to propose another religion: "I am not proposing a religion, but rather the emancipation of elements and outlooks that may be called religious."[35] The freeing of the religious qualities of experience from any object or any intellectual assent is well expressed in the following statement: "The positive lesson is that religious qualities and values if they are real at all are not bound up with any single item of intellectual assent, not even that of the existence of the God of theism."[36] Thus it is clear why Dewey calls anything other than the actual religious aspect of the experience itself to be "a load" added to the experience as excess baggage. He says: "For the moment we have a religion, whether that of the Sioux Indian or of Judaism or of Christianity, that moment the ideal factors in experience that may be called religious take on a load that is not inherent in them, a load of current beliefs and of institutional practices that are irrelevant to them."[37]

Dewey has clearly indicated the possibility of extricating the religious qualities of experience even from the belief in God, not to mention from the further beliefs and practices

---

34. John Dewey, *A Common Faith* (New Haven: Yale University Press, 1971), p. 10.
35. Dewey, p. 8.
36. Dewey, p. 32.
37. Dewey, pp. 8–9.

within a commitment. However, Dewey has gone further than this analysis can allow. While it is necessary to admit that the religious should not be essentially tied to a God belief, especially at the beginning of an analysis of fundamental dimensions, it is equally necessary at this stage to admit that the religious should not be essentially tied to a God nonbelief. Either option should be allowed for at this point, without excluding the possibility of the other. The initial focus on James and Dewey was intended to preserve that possibility at the starting point of this analysis of the fundamental level of religious experience.

Dewey must therefore be seen in the present context to have overstated the case in a way similar to that of James where he seems to limit firsthand religion to cases of the originators and founders of religions and of religious movements. For Dewey, the opposition between religion and the religious values is such that the release of the values is necessary for them even to be viable. "The opposition between religious values as I conceive them and religion is not to be bridged. Just because the release of these values is so important their identification with the creeds and cults of religions must be dissolved."[38] However, it must be admitted and stressed that most reflections of this nature underplay Dewey's position because the prejudice in religious writings is usually already set in the positive option about God, religion and religious experience.

ADJUSTMENT AND ITS OBJECT

James's view of the correlation between the belief and adjustment on the one hand, and the object of religious experience on the other hand, has already been mentioned. For James, the belief in the unseen order and response of adjustment to it are central dimensions of

---

38. Dewey, p. 28.

religious experience, especially as he deals with it in the heart of *The Varieties of Religious Experience.* The following passage draws this out further, allowing us to turn to Dewey's account for possible correlation.

> Were one asked to characterize the life of religion in the broadest and most general terms possible, one might say that it consists of the beliefs that there is an unseen order and that our supreme good lies in harmoniously adjusting ourselves thereto. This belief and this adjustment are the religious attitude in the soul. I wish during this hour to call your attention to some of the psychological peculiarities of such an attitude as this, or belief in an object which we cannot see. All our attitudes, moral, practical or emotional, as well as religious, are due to the "objects" of our consciousness, the things which we believe to exist, whether really or ideally, along with ourselves."[39]

This correlation between the object and the attitude in religious experience differs vastly in the respective views of James and Dewey. While for James the unseen order as the object of belief and adjustment enters into the religious attitude in the soul, for Dewey the correlation between such an object and a response does not induce such a metaphysical assent to "the reality of the unseen." The correlation, in Dewey's view, similar to that of James, *does* include the relation between the object and the belief and adjustment. However, the correlation is between ideals believed and a faith adjustment as response. For Dewey the adjustment to these ideals, springing from the religious attitude, is a change *of* will, and not merely a change *in* will.[40]

Such an adjustment is unique in that it pertains to "our being in its entirety" rather than to "this and that want in relation to this and that condition of our surroundings."[41] Further, this adjustment is all-pervasive, longlasting and

---

39. James, p. 59.
40. Dewey, p. 17.
41. Dewey, p. 116.

enduring, harmonizing all elements of our being, even in relation to changes in the conditions around us. It is a submissive voluntary adjustment or attitude of *faith*, involving a fundamental reorientation of *willing*, taking will "as the organic plenitude of our being."[42] Although not explicit, this is the context in which the adjustment of the total self in relation to the ideals, which bring about the harmony of the self and the universe as an imaginative projection, takes place. "I should describe *this faith* as the *unification* of the self through allegiance to inclusive ideal ends, which imagination presents to us and to which the *human will* responds as worthy of controlling our desires and choices."[43]

The ideals which Dewey treats are important since they are the *imaginatively projected object* of religious adjustment or attitude. These ideals, as such, are not merely figments of imagination. Rather, they emerge and are projected in terms of the concrete situation of life. Imagination, projecting the ideals and aims, does so in terms of possibilities in the universe: "The new vision does not arise out of nothing, but emerges through seeing, in terms of possibilities, that is, of imagination, old things in new relations serving a new end and which the new end aids in creating."[44] As such, though, it is an ongoing process, and never closed. These ideals influence our action, in that they exert a force upon us. In the long run, it is this aspect of ongoing process which influences adjustment having religious qualities. The faith in the possible is liberation from the fixation on the actual, giving rise to the power of the ideal. "All possibilities, as possibilities, are ideal in character."[45] The power of ideals in the religious context are inclusive enough to unify the self, even in harmony

---

42. Dewey, p. 29.
43. Dewey, p. 33.
44. Dewey, p. 49.
45. Dewey, p. 23.

with the universe.[46] That sense of the imaginatively projected ideal of the unity of self and harmony of the universe, as having force on us, indicates the all-pervasiveness of the religious aspect of experience.

> Were the naturalistic foundations and bearings of religion grasped, the religious element in life would emerge from the throes of the crises in religion. Religion would then be found to have its natural place in every aspect of human experience that is concerned with estimate of possibilities, with emotional stir by possibilities as yet unrealized, and with all action in behalf of their realization. All that is significant in human experience falls within this frame.[47]

It must be asked at this point about the value, for a phenomenology of religious experience, of such an analysis of Dewey. In analyzing religious experience in the treatments of both James and Dewey, this study has carefully avoided allowing certain aspects of religious experience to be considered essential at the outset. This study of James's and Dewey's views of religious experience, its object, and its adjustment, make a positive demand on the initial focus: that this focus on religious experience not exclude at the outset by presupposition insights from Dewey's views, especially in relating the religious response to a faith in the power of ideals projected in an ongoing, continuous way. Such a phenomenology, not beginning with a definition of religious experience, can at least accept a warning from Dewey's view of religious experience and not prematurely move into and work within a theistic option. By the same token, it must equally avoid the presupposition of atheism. If phenomenology, as descriptive interpretation, is to be the method, and if its initial change of focus is carefully carried out in keeping with the above stated need for caution, then it is possible now to turn to the analysis of religious experience as it is lived through.

---

46. Dewey, pp. 22–23.
47. Dewey, p. 57.

CHAPTER TWO

Phenomenology of Religious Experience

This chapter will employ phenomenological analysis to ferret out the essential dimensions and structures of certain well-known cases of religious experience. Within this kind of analysis, any experience—as an experience *of* something—can be described only by focusing first on what, in the experience, is the object of the acts which give rise to it. Such an analysis first finds the constitutive correlation between the object within the experience and the whole set of acts and existential conditions which give rise to and make possible this object dimension. Further, this reflective analysis can then move from the object side within the experience to its correlated act or set of acts and to the existential conditions making the experience possible and giving rise to it.

In undertaking this task of phenomenology, the findings of the previous chapter must be employed since the contrast between James and Dewey on the theme of religious experience, the object of its faith, and the adjustment involved in it serve as a guide for initiating the focus of the inquiry. Yet, heeding the warning from the previous chapter not to begin with an assumed interpretation of the status of the object within such an experience, the correlation between the object and the response to it is precisely what must be approached, even though these cases explicitly and specifically interpret that object side. In the context of the above treatments of James and Dewey, an attempt will be made to find, within the contrasting interpretations of the object side of religious experience, what ultimately is essential to such experience. The need to be attentive to the warning will serve to test certain claims about the essentially religious element in experience and in existence.

It cannot be determined at this point whether the religious dimension of human experience is essential to human existence, or whether Dewey's option to retain the religious qualities, attitude, or adjustment within a moral commitment is religious. It has already been seen that, in first approaching the content or object within religious experience, arbitrariness can lead to indefensible omissions: some would eliminate at the outset Dewey's interpretation of the religious and its object, while others similarly would eliminate the Jamesian interpretation of the object. In overcoming or undercutting such arbitrariness, the guiding question in the present investigation would be: is there something essential to the object side or to the content of religious experience lacking in the object side or content of the cases to be studied; or, in this focus, is there something lacking in the interpretations of Dewey and James concerning instances of religious experience as possible imaginative variations? A further question seeks to discover whether there is something not essential to this object side or content but which is considered essential to it.

In entertaining such questions, this study is not concerned with validating the truth claims of the objects of particular religious experiences. It is precisely to question the validity of the assumption that certain aspects of such experiences are essential to human existence that these analyses will be undertaken, and to establish the limits of a phenomenological approach, especially with regard to the object of religious experiences.

However, it must be affirmed at this point that if there is a God, (and this cannot be assumed), then God, as the Jamesian primal reality, could touch the person of religious experience internally, immediately, and on any level of function, as an object of understanding, of willing, of imagination, of the senses, or of affection in the way in

35

which the mystics have often claimed. A person can be thought of as being touched through such objects as the Divine Mother, Jesus, or a powerful presence, etc. It can be seen that to some extent this object could be experienced according to what object is expected as the object of such an experience. On the other hand, if there is no God (and this likewise cannot be assumed), then the ideal projected from the imagination can indeed touch the person in the manner Dewey describes, and these instances of religious experience to be studied here would have to be reinterpreted within another context alien to the interpretations given by those who underwent the experiences and also by those who accepted the accounts of their experiences. Indeed, within either the theistic or the atheistic options, even Dewey's position could be viable, if adapted and appropriated within the theistic option, but with a certain Deweyan limit. It is now to some particular cases of religious experience that the analysis will proceed.

TWO CASES OF RELIGIOUS EXPERIENCE

This reflection will begin by focusing on two familiar cases commonly agreed to be cases of religious experience: the conversion account of Paul the Apostle taken from chapter nine of the *Acts of the Apostles*,[1] and the account of Augustine's conversion experience taken from Book 8 of his *Confessions*.[2] These two cases, although arbitrarily chosen from a wide sweep of possible cases, are chosen for this analysis both because they are well-known and because they so clearly present certain common aspects of conversion experience and, at the same time, present a contrast with one another on certain aspects of religious experience.

---

1. The New American Bible, Acts of the Apostles, 9: 1–20.
2. *The Confessions of St. Augustine*, translated by Edward B. Pusey, D.D (Washington Square Press, Inc.: New York, 1966).

It is clear that a phenomenological analysis could well begin with any one case and vary it in imagination to the point where it clearly ceases to be a case of this type of experience. Such an imaginative variation can proceed by varying this one case to ascertain its essential structure or, in other words, vary it to find those dimensions or conditions without which the experience would not be what it is.[3] Hence, such variation does not remain limited to a treatment of one case, although that would certainly be viable. It can proceed by focusing on several cases, each taken as an imaginative variation of the general type, religious experience. In following this procedure, the various cases are then taken as already given variations in contrast with one another, and the analysis proceeds by way of finding the essential dimensions which defy variation and which necessarily must be present in the experience for it to still be what it is. The nonessential dimensions then begin to appear as such and can be put off precisely *as* not essential to the case.

It is the precise variation between the first two cases to be considered which begins this discussion concerning what is essential to religious experience. In addition, other cases, either familiar to the general reader or deliberately fabricated as familiar to everyone's experience, will further highlight differences and variations among instances of religious experience. Thus, this focus throws into more forceful focus the common elements or the essential structures, since the differences can be seen in an essential common structure. It is precisely this structure which the analysis of these different cases of religious experience is attempting to grasp explicitly.

---

3. Although phenomenology can proceed by varying a case in such a way as to ascertain what elements or characteristics are essential to it, the present employment of the method will be a variation of that technique. Instead of simply varying a particular case, a different and contrasting case will be used to pose the question of what is essential to religious

The conversion of Paul the Apostle to Christianity and the accompanying circumstances are well-known and therefore only require a brief treatment. He was on his way from Jerusalem to Damascus with letters in hand empowering

> him to arrest and bring to Jerusalem anyone he might find, man or woman, living according to the new way. As he traveled along and was approaching Damascus, a light from the sky suddenly flashed about him. He fell to the ground and at the same time heard a voice saying: "Saul, Saul, why do you persecute me?" "Who are you, sir?" he asked. The voice answered. "I am Jesus, the one you are persecuting. Get up and go into the city, where you will be told what to do." The men who were traveling with him stood there speechless. They had heard the voice but could see no one. Paul got up from the group unable to see, even though his eyes were open. They had to take him by the hand and lead him into Damascus. For three days he continued blind, during which time he neither ate nor drank.[4]

In the context of interpreting this as a case of the religious experience of conversion, the fact should be emphasized that Paul is someone who, prior to his conversion to Christianity, hated and persecuted Christians. Yet, in spite of this adversarial attitude, after this experience Paul did not even question whether it was indeed Christ whom he experienced. Further, it is to be noted that the experience included something experienced from outside himself, as is often the case in such experiences. This is especially manifest in the light and in the voice, which, as seen in the narration, emerge from outside and are experienced by others present.

From this event, together with his baptism and consequent experiences, Paul's whole life was changed; he became an avid Christian, integrating his prior Jewish

---

experience among the differences of various cases, thus capitalizing on the variation among cases which are well-known.

4. Acts of the Apostle, 9: 2–9.

experiences, heritage and commitment around the experience of Christ, and eventually becoming a preacher and an apostle. It is clear that Paul did not respond out of a void of religious life, for he had been a fanatic in his prior faith commitment. Now, although completely changed, his commitment for Christ was equally forceful.

It can be seen, then, that there is in this later faith a commitment to Christ, and that it is from this faith in Christ that his response emanates. The basic structure of the experience as religious is the personal presence of a religious object, Jesus Christ, who was experienced in a strange and unique fashion. It is precisely the basic structure of such an experience which must be investigated in order to find out if that structure is all-pervasive and essential to all cases of religious experience.

In turning at this point to Augustine's conversion experience, focusing on the one event which highlighted an already well-developed path of conversion, a further dimension of the basic structure of religious experience can be revealed in a different light, using this instance as an imaginative variation. In this case, Augustine has been living as on a quest, searching in philosophies and religious expressions of the day for something which could satisfy him. His mother had been praying and hoping for years that he would accept the Christian faith, which he had resisted and refused. At the end of Book 8 of his *Confessions*, Augustine relates how he was in the garden with his friend Alypius discussing in great anguish these matters which were of such concern to him, when he fled to another part of the garden to be alone.[5]

> So was I speaking and weeping in the most bitter contrition of my heart, when, lo: I heard from a neighboring house voices of boy or girl, I know not, chanting, and oft repeating, "take up and read!" Instantly, my countenance altered, I began to think most intently whether children were

---

5. *The Confessions of St. Augustine*, pp. 147–148.

wont in any kind of play to sing such words: nor would I remember ever to have heard the like. So checking the torrent of my tears, I arose; interpreting it to be no other than a command from God to open the book, and read the first chapter I should find. For I had heard of Anthony, that coming in during the reading of the Gospel, he received the admonition, as if what was being read was spoken to him: Go, sell all that thou hast and give to the poor, and thou shalt have treasure in heaven, and come and follow me: and by such oracle he was forthwith converted unto Thee. Eagerly then I returned to the place where Alypius was sitting; for there had I laid the volume of the Apostle when I arose thence. I seized, opened, and in silence read that section on which my eyes first fell. Not in rioting and drunkenness, not in chambering and wantonness, not in strife and envying but put ye on the Lord Jesus Christ and make not provision for the flesh in concupiscence. No further would I read: nor needed I: for instantly at the end of this sentence by a light as it were of serenity infused into my heart all the darkness of doubt vanished away.

The experiences of Christ undergone by both Paul and Augustine are emotionally intense and involve a response of faith and an adjustment. There are some shades of difference in the basic accounts of each of these experiences, especially relating to the adjustment response. This difference must be further analyzed, but only after some reflection on the object side and the content of each experience.

OBJECT SIDE OF THE EXPERIENCE

In each of these cases, Jesus Christ is considered to be experienced as real and alive in some way. These experiences of Christ thus elicited bring about a response indicating that the person is someone special, in this case, the central figure of a religion. Each of the individuals undergoing the experiences was aware of the special claims constituting a certain uniqueness of Christ. It is precisely this uniqueness of Christ within the typically religious dimension of the sect in Paul's day which made him so adamantly opposed to these Christians, since he considered theirs to be an heretical religious belief deviating from his strict Jewish beliefs. Augustine, likewise, throughout the whole context which led to and climaxed in this conversion experience, was aware of the specifically religious character of the person of Christ in which the Christians believed. In their responses to this person experienced in these two accounts, it is precisely and unquestioningly to Christ as a religious figure to whom they each responded. However the Old Testament themes applied to Christ by the early church are interpreted, the fact is that a certain religious ultimacy belongs to each of these accounts, and is clearly involved in that to which both Augustine and Paul responded. Neither of them questioned whether it was indeed Christ, nor whether it was possible to be touched by someone supposedly dead to an existence lived by earthly mortals on earth. Somehow Christ was taken to be alive and relevant to their lives. Within the context of his proclaiming the kingdom of God as prophet, priest and victim, Christ also was considered to have something to do with the fundamental tradition of Judaism and Christianity and, thus, to be uniquely related to the divine. He was seen to have some special relation to an ultimacy in being or in the object of religious faith. It is precisely this aspect of ultimacy[6] in the object of the faith to which one commits himself that gives the object side of this experience its unique significance. If Christ had been just another person who had no special significance, there would not have been any special dimension to this experience.

One element must be further clarified. The fact that

---

6. In order to avoid equivocation in the use of the term "ultimacy," it is necessary to repeat that the use of this term throughout this study is not limited to the sense of an ultimate being or object. See note 4 in Chapter One.

Christ had been dead for some time enters into each of these cases as an important factor. Yet one can ask also whether the experiences of those around Christ during his life can be said to have been religious experiences. In other words, is it essential to the experience of him that he be dead, yet manifest? Or, is it the case that those who experienced him in his real physical presence could likewise be said to experience something unique about him which made it a religious experience? Since Christ in his own life did indeed engage in a work of preaching the arrival of the kingdom, and was interpreted in a certain role with certain titles, at least some of those who experienced him often responded in a conversion, faith and baptism response and, indeed, must be considered likewise to have undergone a religious experience similar to those of Paul and Augustine. The specific claims and preaching of Christ set him apart as someone special, with a certain relation to God, and thus revealed what was called above an aspect of ultimacy. This aspect of ultimacy is not meant to capture the essence of his claim, since the aim of this analysis is to find what is essential, not to Christian experiences, but to that experience understood simply as an instance of religious experience. Therefore, this could be considered common to similar objects in other experiences occurring in other religious contexts.

The focal point in any account of these and similar experiences is the acceptance on the part of the one undergoing the experience that the object of his faith, even if just acquired, is indeed something with a special relation to ultimacy or, in other words, to God, or to the transcendent. It is this character of the God-transcedent-ultimacy which will be seen to appear in the cases to be studied later. For now, some further comments concerning the ultimacy and transcendence in the context of phenomenology require further reflection and integration.

Phenomenology employs the use of the term "transcendent"[7] in a broader sense than the religious use of Transcendent as the ultimate object of religious believers. The possibility of equivocating can be avoided in a brief consideration of the meaning and function of the transcendent in the constitution of all human experience. Phenomenology contends that a certain transcendence constitutes any concrete experience of any object, whether it be the experience in the perception of an object, or the experience in thinking of a mathematical objectivity. In this sense, the content of the particular experience, the object experienced in perception or in thinking, is seen to go beyond the particular functions or acts in which it is for the present moment sustained. In this sense, it is said to transcend the particular act or acts which give rise to it. Thus, since the object transcends any particular acts within the object-subject correlation within the lived experience, it can be said to transcend those acts and even the particular conditions of the particular, lived experience. Further, such experiences of objects and of objectivities can be experienced objectively at another time by the same person or by other persons. Likewise, meanings can be said to transcend the particular event or situation of their emergence into lived experience. Although it must be admitted that the object of religious experience has a correlation to transcendence, it need not be affirmed at this point to be more than this general transcendence, and therefore indicates basically an

---

7. This treatment of transcendence simply shows the equivocation involved in the uses of the term, without entering into the esoteric discussion among phenomenologists about the relation between intentionality and transcendence, or about the ontic and ontological senses of transcendence. Although most of the discussion on these matters has been deliberately postponed, it may be helpful to indicate at this point that the ontological aspect of transcendence is the foundation of the ontic, in the sense of these terms developed in Chapter Three. Ontological transcendence is the foundation for ontic transcendence, which, in turn, is constituted by intentionality. Further, the sense of the Transcendent as absolute is not at all part of the discussion of ontic or ontological transcendence. These issues will be explicitly discussed in the ensuing chapters.

openness of the experience to it. But it is an experience of transcendence, with the character of ultimacy in the object experienced, and this object is the object of a faith commitment including—at least in the two cases dealt with above— a reality or existence status.

Further, this transcendent object, with its character of ultimacy in relation to a God, as the object side of the religious experience, cannot be merely the horizon of such experiences and of all other experiences, as has often been considered to be the case. This horizon of experience is not adequate to the specificness of such objects of religious experience as Jesus Christ, the Divine Love, the Presence, the Divine Mother, etc. It must be further noted that to add, at this point in the analysis, the being or divine character as specific to the objective correlate of religious experience is to claim more than the experience can justify, and this fails to account for the variation among objects giving rise to similar religious experience unless it is admitted that the objects, even in their differences and variations, do have in common a claim to ultimacy for the individual, even though in analysis this ultimacy appears undetermined.

Dealing with the ultimacy and transcendence of the object side of religious experience in the context of the imaginative variation afforded by the analyses of Dewey leads to further insight about the limit to the essential claim of the object side. This character of ultimacy can be seen to be derived from the object, such as Christ or the Divine Mother. It can equally be seen to be a characteristic of the object side of the imaginatively projected ideal, according to which we can guide our lives to their utmost moral heights by seeing the possibilities latent in our situation. Dewey's ideal as object has already been seen to contain ultimacy[8] in the harmony and unity of self and the universe as an imaginative projection.

---

8. This is the very loosest sense of ultimacy, since it can in no way make Dewey's view of values and ideals rigid and inflexible.

Although Dewey's assumption with regard to the religious option is diametrically opposed to that of the religious person, it has been seen to have the same roots: i.e., the volitional passional nature of man. Dewey's naturalism begins with no transcendent metaphysical object or being as supernatural, entering rather into an option which excludes that possibility. Dewey, just as do James and others, works within such an option without apodictic evidence. The roots of such an option reach into the entire person, including the cognitive, the volitional and passional dimensions.

It is the precise aim of this study to undercut either option insofar as the essential dimensions of religious experience cannot be fairly assumed to be accessible in only one of these options, as has been clearly raised as a question in the context of dealing with Dewey's account of the religious aspect of experience and existence. In attempting to overcome any such prejudice at the outset in appropriating phenomenological method to reflect philosophically on religious experience, letting the experience speak for itself has revealed that it is limited in what it can say on its own.

Within the claim to ultimacy in general, no specification of the object need be stipulated for analysis. However, from within the experience itself, the assumed faith framework or the option in general is the context within which further specifications of the object are added. The ultimacy itself can be considered to include constitutive contributions from the overall gamut of human experience, such as the affective, the practical and the cognitive dimensions. Further, this ultimacy is implicitly lived, so that an unfolding of values constituting human life emerges with its ultimacy. It must be admitted, nevertheless, that the character of ultimacy could be merely finite, as it is considered to be in Dewey's value system. Consequently, ultimacy as a character, phenomenologically derivable from accounts of religious experience, does not militate against the interpretation of ultimacy in the structures of human experience and existence as finite in orientation. Yet a religious experience loses something essential if ultimacy is not present in it.

Thus, this characterization of ultimacy as present is essential to the experience. Ultimacy is neutral to the conflicting claims of various types of religious experience, and to the claims of varying second level, reflective analyses. The precise sense in which this characteristic of the object of religious experience can be considered essential to human experience in general and to human existence is what must be seen in the discussion in following chapters. It is to the noetic elements of religious experience that the discussion will now turn.

EXPERIENCING THE OBJECT

Although each of the experiences mentioned above can be seen to involve an adjustment constituted in part by the noetic aspect of the experience, it must be admitted that Paul, in the confusion of the events, was already operating within an intense religious response and adjustment prior to the conversion narrated in this account. Augustine, by contrast, was converted from a completely different frame of mind, one in which he was searching for something, but not within an intense religious adjustment response. This variation does not exclude the essentially religious characters of either of these accounts, but simply shows that one case involves a revamping of an already given adjustment response, while the other involves the emrgence of such an adjustment. In spite of such a variation between these two cases of religious experience, whether the experience initiates the appropriation of a religious life or simply falls within such an already achieved adjustment, they both are considered to be instances of religious experience—at least to the extent that they contain the essential dimensions of a religious response of a faith and an adjustment to something as ultimate, as was seen to be required in the accounts of both James and Dewey. What is seen clearly here is the need to consider religious experience as including instances which go far beyond those cases which bring about the initial religious commitment and an ensuing life differing from that before the experience. These cases do not challenge the essential role of adjustment but, rather, relate religious experience to such an adjustment to be initiated or to be readjusted in a different response, sustained unchanged and continuous throughout the experience. In this case there is simply intense experience, rather than conversion in the Jamesian sense.

In the cases of such mystics as Teresa of Avila, the mystical experiences take place within an adjustment which is already there without leading to a recasting of the initial adjustment, as in the case of Paul. In such cases, therefore, the experience can be seen to emerge from and to take place within an adjustment, but one which encompasses a whole religious life. Even this experience, however, involves an adjustment, since without such an adjustment as seen in the studies of James and Dewey, the religious experience would not be possible, and would not be a case of religious experience.

In spite of the above variations, afforded by different cases, whether the experience initiates the appropriation of a religious life (as in the case of Augustine), or changes such an appropriation (as in the case of Paul), or simply falls within such an already achieved adjustment (as in the case of Teresa of Avila), they are to be considered religious experiences at least to the extent that they would not be challenged by most people on the subject. Therefore, although such a profound, voluntary and enduring adjustment is essential to religious experience, it would be narrow to say that each religious experience must lead essentially to initiate such a religious adjustment, since many admittedly religious experiences take place within an adjustment already appropriated. Such an adjustment is essential to all these variations of religious experience, and must be considered part of its structure, whether the particular experience leads to an adjustment, or emerges in one way or another from it. This adjustment, then, is constitutive of the experience so far considered to be religious.

Yet, in considering these cases of Augustine, Paul, and mystics such as Teresa of Avila, the question must be posed: how or in what sense is adjustment essential to the experience? Is it the case that without it, there would be no religious experience? This is a question involving the subject side of the religious experience. Further, it is a question fundamental to phenomenological technique, asking what is it without which this would not be an instance of religious experience. Would this be a religious experience without adjustment?

The adjustment seems to belong essentially to the response precisely *as* religious, because without it the response would not be considered religious. Without the adjustment element, each of these cases mentioned would be so radically changed that they could not be considered instances of genuine religious experience. In the case of Paul, the adjustment undergirded his whole active life prior to the conversion experience, and the readjustment after that event of conversion brought about a wholly different life. With Teresa, the adjustment, already the context for her life, was the foundation for the whole life of prayer about which she speaks so much. The adjustment in the cases of Paul and Teresa was the presupposed foundation or condition for the experience, in that—without it—no such experience would have been possible unless such an adjustment was evoked in the experiences, as in the case of Augustine. It might be added that even in such a case as that of Augustine, in which the adjustment is initiated through the experience and then becomes the person's religious response for an enduring period, the adjustment has been foundational in that it did not happen in a flash. He was somewhat prepared by his own personal searching and desperate condition. It is possible, however, as has been accounted in other variations of religious experience, that an event of conversion can indeed bring about the adjustment without any seeming preparation, and the adjustment can emerge once and for all in a profound and evocative experience.

EXPERIENCING THE OBJECT: ANOTHER CASE

The preceding variation in the characteristic of adjustment involved in religious experience brings to attention the possibility of a further variation involving a case of what James calls secondhand religious experience without firsthand religious experience.[9] Unless this case is excluded at the outset from the set of religious experiences, it might challenge certain usually accepted aspects of the adjustment response. This variation questions the relation between the adjustment response and the religious attitude or experience of those whom James calls "secondhand" religionists, those without religious experience at the heart of their religious lives. Since these cases are not intense, they are usually not considered to be cases of religious experience. Thus, the variation involves questioning whether these are cases of religious experience continuing what is necessarily essential to religious experience, or questioning whether something essential to religious experience as such has been eliminated in them. This type of case requires further analysis.

All the Christian religions obviously include individuals limited to this kind of religious experience. It is a case of people who do believe in God, and in religious practices and doctrines, but usually without feeling, emotion, warmth or firsthand experience. This seems to be a response containing all of the Deweyian "load" or excess baggage. Usually church services are not enjoyed by such

---

9. It will be recalled that in Chapter One the relation between emotion and religious experience was explicitly treated.

individuals, but often it is the case that they would not miss them, especially in those religious denominations which demand such attendance. The whole practice is determined by beliefs. Living up to these beliefs involves a practice or religion in the sense that it goes far beyond a mere theoretical assent to God's existence. This is, of course, a case of more than merely a cultural religious expression in which there is hardly any religious belief. For such people would probably defend their belief, even die for it, although they probably have not thought of it. They believe in God, the reward after death, duty to live a morally upright life and, in their own way, a love of God. James seems to exclude explicitly this case from those he considers in the firsthand religious experience, which is the focus of his interest in *The Varieties of Religious Experience*. Thus, with this case, what is essentially challenged is the tendency in James to dichotomize firsthand and secondhand religious experiences.

As a Response of the Whole Person

In cases of secondhand religious experience the belief is more than merely a theoretical, intellectual assent. This is clear from the effective response elicited in the practice of religion for such individuals whose response involves a whole context of lived experience, even though different from cases usually referred to as cases of religious experience. This response is therefore not reducible to sheer naked intellectual assent and ritual practice in that, taking those away, a certain element of the response remains which is related to practice. As a practice of religion, there is an in-depth practical adjustment, involving commitment of will, freedom and responsibility which is not simply reducible to a moral response. This response includes the response of a total person, i.e., freedom, emotion and awareness, even though it is not an intense response. It can be seen to be a response of the whole person, includ-

50

ing the theoretical, practical and affective aspects of human experience, but not a hot flash kind of experience with emotional intensity. Certain personal aspects are manifest and constitute the fullness of the response. For such practice is pulled forward or elicited with some feeling of prior or consequent security, of comfort, of obligation, or of respect, love, fear, etc. Although such people may not "feel" the presence of God, they have feelings involved at the gut level of the response and expressed in practice. At least to some extent and in some way, God's presence can be assumed to be involved in their faith. It is not, however, the feeling of God's presence which is the feeling indicated above, but rather, the feeling involved at the gut level of the response expressed in their practice which is a necessary dimension of the response. Nevertheless, regarding the element of feeling essential to such a response, a qualification is necessary. This qualification can be analyzed via Dewey's view of the relation between emotion and the religious aspect of experience.

For Dewey, there is a complete adjustment which necessarily includes an emotional element, and which sets this response to a certain type of ideal apart from a merely ethical ideal. He says: "What has been said does not imply that all moral faith in ideal ends is by virtue of that fact religious in quality. The religious is 'morality touched by emotion' only when the ends of moral conviction arouse emotions that are not only intense but are actuated and supported by ends so inclusive that they unify the self." Dewey later defines this moral faith: "I should describe this faith as the unification of the self through allegiance to inclusive ends, which imagination presents to us and to which the human will respond as worthy of controlling our desires and choices."[10] He states further: "The self is always directed toward something beyond itself and so its own unification depends upon the idea of the integration of the shifting scenes of the world into that imaginative

---

10. Dewey, *A Common Faith*, p. 33.

totality we call the universe."[11] Dewey wants to avoid identifying the ideal with a particular Being. Rather, these ideals and aims "which move us" arise from the imagination, and emerge "through seeing, in terms of possibilities, that is, of imagination, old things in new relations serving a new end which the new end aids in creating."[12] Then, he says that "an unseen power controlling our destiny becomes the power of an ideal."[13]

We have invoked Dewey's view of the religious in experience according to which all intellectual beliefs are excess baggage and extraneous to religious experience understood as morality with intense emotion.[14] Further, according to that view, an imaginatively projected ideal as the force eliciting an attitude of adjustment ultimately can bring about the unity of the self and of the universe. Dewey rejects the one object or being of religious experience, but still defines religious experience in terms of or as including intense emotion.

Returning to the type of case involving the apathetic response, can we say (of the religious experience practiced in that variation) that feeling only accompanies the practice and is not an essential part of it, as in the case of the feelings simply accompanying the practice of mathematical thinking, and have no essential relation to it? This could be thought to be the case in sheer, naked belief in God's existence, but even here, the roots of that belief are more than merely an assent of intellect, since such belief has been seen to be rooted in the volitional passional nature of man.

All that has been affirmed thus far is that *feeling* necessarily enters into the constitution of the religious experience as part of its meaning structure, and therefore is

---

11. Dewey, p. 19.
12. Dewey, p. 49.
13. Dewey, p. 23.
14. Dewey, p. 22.

constitutive of the experience. This does not mean that there is any one or more special religious feelings, i.e. there is not a special feeling which can be called religious. What this analysis has brought to light is that religious experience expresses essentially the realm of feeling in some practical commitment, implicitly including some kinds of intellectual content even if perhaps only the awareness of ideals projected. Further, it includes in some way the total realms of experience of the whole person and thus is all-inclusive of various aspects of human functioning. Therefore, religious experience can be seen to be a response including the total individual, even when it is not a "total" response. This is seen to be at odds with those who, like Dewey, include as essential to such an experience the intensity of emotion. For the essential aspects of such an experience have been seen in this analysis to be the ultimacy of the object and the response of the whole person.

So the significance of the case of the apathetic religious response clearly emerges. It requires the extension of the notion of religious experience and its adjustment to undercut the dichotomy between secondhand religion and firsthand religious experience. What has become apparent is that at least in the type of case cited, there is also a firsthand element in the adjustment response. Thus cases of this type do fall under the label of religious experience.

CONCLUSION

A phenomenology of religious experience can be seen to reveal ultimacy as a character of the object side of religious experience. This ultimacy survives the imaginative variations of the object or of the various objects of the same or of different religious experiences. Ultimacy is therefore the characteristic essential to the object side of religious experience. To call this ultimacy "God," however, or an absolute "being" in the supernatural sense is to claim more than the descriptive interpretation of this dimension of religious experience can account for, thus yielding more than is essential to religious experience as such. Ultimacy, as belonging essentially or eidetically to experience, considered from the religious perspective, is as essential to the Deweyian religious qualities of experience as it is to the accounts of the Sacred in the variations of manifestations depicted in various religions. A phenomenology of religious experience finds itself having to admit that Dewey cannot be disproved by means of a phenomenological account of religious experience, which gives his theory equal claims to the essential dimensions descriptively uncovered. However, Dewey's naturalism, as well as James's supernaturalism, begins within an already made option concerning God. Further, the recent attempts at a phenomenological analysis of the religious by such scholars as Langdon Gilkey[15] give rise to a suspicion that they, too, take place within such an option. But Dewey and James or Gilkey begin within opposite options. A phenomenology of religious experience, although quite valid and enlightening for the religious person or theologian, does not justify an initial assumption of theism. The phenomenological return to the experience itself is found to limit claims made from that experience, for it is neutral to the conflicting claims of various types of religious experience, and to the claims of varying second-level reflective analyses. Such phenomenological analyses are not able to deny or to justify any such post-option claims, not even the God belief of a fundamental option, indicating that such experience is not self-validating.

The religious response of the religious subject, constituting the subject side of religious experience, involves the whole person in such a way as to include the realm of feeling in some practical commitment implicitly including

---

15. See note 2 of Chapter One.

the total functioning of the human being, even when it is not a total response. The full phenomenological analysis of religious experience, taking both the subject and the object poles into account, reveals religious experience to be constituted by an adjustment involving the whole person— theoretical, practical and affective—in a response to an object within experience regarded as having ultimacy.

CHAPTER THREE

Existential Dimensions of
Religious Experience

This chapter attempts to delve beneath religious experience to its ground in existence. The understanding of the fundamental level of lived experience and of the lived world emerges in the context of existence as the root and as the presuppositional context for all levels and structures of experience. In changing the focus from the structural aspects of religious experience, seen in the previous chapter, to its existential roots, a twofold distinction is helpful. First, the structure of religious experience, constituted by a structure common to all experience, is to be investigated in the context of horizontal and vertical dimensions of experience in general. Second, in considering experience in its existential roots, a distinction between the ontic and the ontological dimensions of existence must be made. The variations in the concrete manners and styles of existence, as ontic aspects of being-in-the-world, can be analyzed in terms of ontological dimensions common to any ontic mode of concrete existence. It is to the first of these themes, the relation of religious experience as a specific kind of experience to the horizontal and vertical aspects of experience in general, that the discussion must now turn briefly.

Religious experience has been seen to be a religious response involving the whole person in such a way as to include the realm of feeling in some practical commitment implicitly including the total human existent, even when it is not a total or intense response. A phenomenological analysis of religious experience, taking both the subject and the object poles into account, has revealed religious experience to be constituted by an adjustment involving a response to an object present within experience which is regarded as having ultimacy. This understanding of religious experience can be brought to greater explicitness and depth if integrated with an understanding of the various levels of experience in general.

Deepening the understanding of religious experience to include the relation between its horizontal and vertical structures reveals a more complete context for the treatment of its horizontal structure, which was treated in the previous chapter. Further analysis of such experience in terms of the correlation between its acts and objects, in terms of its relation to other levels of experience, and especially in terms of more concrete and existential foundations, reveals its involvement within the whole gamut of levels of experience. It is in this context that the horizontal and vertical aspects of experience must be distinguished.

The horizontal aspect of experience simply entails the structure of any experience, for instance, its subject side and object side, rooted in intentionality and in transcendence.[1] Every experience, including religious experience, is constituted by an objectivity or object given rise to within experience by acts of the one who undergoes the experience. Further, this structure of any experience is rooted in the all-pervasive aspect of experience according to which it is wedded to that which is not itself. In other terms, it is constitutively related to that which transcends it as act, such as things, objectivities, beings or being. Experience, consciousness or human being can be seen to go beyond or transcend themselves insofar as they are relational in their constitution. These elements have been seen in the previous phenomenological analysis of religious experience.

---

1. The relation between intentionality and transcendence is extremely important for any phenomenological reflection on experience and existence. The manner in which that relation is read determines the fundamental stance toward the epistemic and the ontological in their correlation. This correlation will be further treated in a later section of this chapter.

The vertical aspect of experience throws into focus the relation between aspects of an experience "above" and "below" it, or, perhaps better described, the relation between higher acts and lower acts. In this context a fundamental contrast must be made between any act in experience and the pre-act level which grounds it. Since the structure of any experience is constituted by intentionality, which is rooted in existence, any such analysis can and should lead in the direction of the analysis of the existential intentionality which underlies particular acts. For below acts of awareness in experience is the level which makes acts possible, i.e., that intentionality which is constitutive of existence as being-in-the-world and from which emerges the already present familiar world in relation to which living or existing transpires.

Religious experience can be seen to take place on the level of acts giving rise to certain objects constitutive of religious experience. However, the response of faith and adjustment, as such, involves more than acts, since the characteristics of these acts have been lead back into fuller and more concrete aspects of the response than is manifest in acts. Thus, the whole person has been seen to be the source of the response, which, when traced back to its roots in the originary level, is found to include a fundamental mode of being-in-the-world or a basic attitude of attunement and adjustment to something. Within the focus on existence, the specific acts contained within a particular response are seen to be drived from and founded on the more basic and existential level of openness of human existence. Considering this existential level leads to the distinction which must be made between the ontic and the ontological dimensions of existence.

Concrete existence as such must be distinguished from its essential, ontological aspects. The human existent as an entity can be considered in reflection from the point of view of its actual concrete conditions and accidental characteristics, its everyday being as an entity existing with other entities. By contrast, human existence can also be considered from the point of view of the underlying structures and sense of its being which are all-pervasive and limited to accidental conditions of concrete existence. A phenomenological approach can look for the underlying dimensions of the concrete conditions. As such, it delves beneath the merely concrete and accidental conditions of an entity to the essential characteristics of its being. In this way, the distinction between the ontic and the ontological dimensions of an entity becomes clear. The ontic aspect bespeaks the concrete entity and its characteristics as such, while the ontological dimension refers to the being-aspects of the entity. The ontological aspect underlies the ontic and is constitutive of the being of the entity in its foundational being-in-the-world. In the present discussion, then, "ontological" means the all-pervasive aspects of an entity.[2]

It has been necessary to make this distinction between the ontic and the ontological in order to understand that the present discussion, for the moment, must remain first on the ontic level and explore the different concrete ways of existing in relation to religious response. The two ways of being religious, theistic and atheistic, must be dealt with first on this ontic level before broadening the scope to include the question of the ontological aspects of human being in terms of the religious aspects of existence.

The transition from the analysis of the structural aspects of religious experience to their existential roots involves the further explication of the fundamental level of lived experience emerging in existence as the presuppositional context for all levels and structures of experience. It is on this concrete level that existence must be taken as the

---

2. This sense of ontological must not be confused with the study of ontology, giving rise to another sense of the word "ontological." In that sense of ontological, the meaning indicates that which pertains in some way to the study of ontology. Although this use of the word ontology refers precisely to the study which unfolds or reveals the ontological aspects of being mentioned above, the two senses are not to be confused.

presuppositional situation and substrate for all experience and thus for religious experience. All philosophical reflection emerges from the prephilosophical level as the presuppositional context for philosophy.

In initiating a phenomenological reflection on the religious dimensions of existence, the above analyses must proceed in a continuous line of development leading through the analysis of religious *experience* to the analysis of religious *existence*. The caution necessary in the initial phenomenological analyses of religious experience must not now be lost in this transition to religious existence. Although it is viable to begin an analysis of religious existence within an option for God and the religious, and within a particular religious tradition or, even more specifically, within a particular denomination or sect with a particular tradition, the option and its presuppositions cannot be allowed to take on an absolute status at the outset. Consequently, at the beginning, the possibility of a neutrality within religious existence toward the status of the specific object of religious experience and existence must be maintained. It is with this in mind that the following analysis delves deeper into the sense of religious existence. It is the contention of this study that religious existence in relation to ultimacy of some object is neutral to theism or atheism: that the religious is a basic dimension of existence, but as such, is neutral to a specific determination of its object. Therefore, it must be seen to what extent the neutrality emerging from a phenomenological analysis of religious experience can be maintained in an analysis led to the concrete existing entity, the person, in the everyday being-in-the-world. An investigation of such possible neutrality requires further clarification of existence as foundational, the level at which the question of neutrality is to be pursued.

It has already been indicated that existence is foundational to consciousness, to perception, to experiences, and to awareness in general as their ground, source and foundation. A comprehension is constitutive of the foundational existence which is already there at the occasion of particular acts which are grounded in it. For instance, in acting in the worlds of fishing, of academia, of business or of athletics, a whole network of meanings is operative and familiar to the one who is engaging in such activity, and so founds such activity. An individual, acting in any one of these particular worlds, is already familiar with the meaning totality of his projected activity. Such familiarity is a trait of human existence. There is a familiarity with entities and their total context in encountering, using or enjoying them. Further, this familiarity with particular worlds of our living can be deepened to the fundamental but concrete world of human experience and existence. All individuals exist in the concrete and, as such, have a particular concrete totality as the context of their existence or as the familiar world of their intercourse. Although many worlds of concrete existence can be indicated, the common denominator is the fact that there is a familiar world in relation to which we carry on life. It is within this context of a concrete being-in-the-world that particular acts or experiences take place.

Carried further, this analysis shows the openness of human existence, in its fundamental meaning, to being itself. Underlying and founding any concrete being-in-the-world, or any possible worlds of our familiarity, and underlying and founding all derived acts and experiences is the awareness of the being of things, of self, of anything and of everything. It is this which can be brought forth in the analysis of any kind of experience. However, in indicating that the openness of existence reveals the being of things, the being of human existence and being in general, it must be indicated that *being* in this context is the being of entities, and not being as an absolute transcendent. That would require an invalid jump from the all-pervasive feature emerging in the experience of entities, and would be an untrue account of experience and of existence.

Within the analysis of religious experience seen in the previous section, the transition to the existential foundations of the experiences analyzed can be seen as an easy one. In the structure of those experiences, constituted by the ultimacy of an object and by the response of faith-adjustment, the experiences can be seen to be clearly rooted in existence. First of all, the faith-adjustment response, although emerging in an experience in some instances, can easily be considered from the point of view of its existential foundations, since the response consists of more than acts. In the case of Augustine, a conversion to Christ from a non religious attitude (although one of searching) demonstrated a response which affected his whole world and his whole response to, or adjustment in, life. His existence was changed. Such an adjustment permeated his concrete being-in-the-world. The same must be said of Paul and of the cases in the other analyses. In Paul's case, although the religious was explicitly operative before the experience, the consequent faith-adjustment response involved a revamping of his world and of his concrete being-in-the-world. In both cases the ultimacy responded to and the faith-adjustment response were altered radically in existence. Every structure and all-pervasive aspect of their concrete existence was permeated by the religious. And in the case of mystics, such as Theresa, the same can be said—but in the context of a whole life and not merely in the context of the consequences of some isolated experience.

In a similar way, the ultimacy in the case of the individual of secondhand religious experience can be seen to be constitutive as a correlate to his existence as religious, since his acts, practices, mores and feelings all emerge from within an existential context which is religious. The response, as one of existential orientation, is seen to be foundational before becoming acts and particular experiences. Therefore, the fundamental awareness of ultimacy, and the response of the whole person to it, emerge as an all-pervasive feature of their concrete existences. The same analysis applies equally to the case of the atheist depicted by Dewey. The ultimacy of the (all-encompassing) ideal and the faith-adjustment response to it are seen to be fundamental to concrete existence and to the being-in-the-world of the individual, and likewise to be all-pervasive features of concrete existence.

The analysis of religious experience undertaken in the previous chapters must be brought to explicate the presuppositional base from which such reflection, and indeed, all reflection, proceeds. Thus, the presuppositional situation for such reflection and the common background for all philosophical reflection is brought to the fore as the point from which it emerges and to which it returns.[3] Certain aspects of this complex presuppositional situation[4] must be elaborated in order to understand the context from which reflection emerges, and in order to avoid the tendency to oversimplify it.

In dealing with the ground for philosophical reflection, the circle involved in understanding must be brought to light so that the implicitly grasped prereflective and pre-philosophical dimensions of existence are brought to explicit philosophical reflection.[5] Great importance must be placed on the explication of presuppositions as bringing to light the ground for reflection and therefore for reflection on religious existence.

As mentioned earlier, the focus of the analysis of human existence as presuppositional can be limited to its ontic aspects in contrast to its ontological aspects.[6] Within such a

---

3. Martin Heidegger, *Being and Time*, translated by John Macquarrie and Edward Robinson, (Max Niemeyer Verlag: Tubingen, 1963), p. 62.

4. Heidegger, pp. 274–278.

5. Heidegger, pp. 182–195.

6. See Gilkey, *Naming the Whirlwind*, pp. 336 and 413, for further treatment of the distinction between the ontic and the ontological. It seems that Gilkey has failed to recognize the implicitly ontological dimension of certain aspects of his so-called ontic claims of the Sacred as the unconditioned.

limit the human existent, simply as an entity, is described as such. This kind of analysis can involve everyday living in a concrete world with its presuppositions, structures and habits, or it can include any or all of many worlds, for instance, the workaday world, the religious world within a belief or commitment, or a particular political world, etc. These various worlds and commitments of everyday concrete existence can come under scrutiny and analysis without their ontological conditions being revealed as such, and without the analysis becoming ontological. This is the claim which such a philosopher-theologian as Langdon Gilkey makes: that his analysis of the Sacred in relation to existence is not ontological, and that the Sacred in the life of the religious person and the Sacred or unconditioned in the implicit aspects of the lived experience of the secularist are not ontological, but rather ontic, as shall be seen.

In order for such an inquiry to become ontological, it must go beyond the ontic level and penetrate to the fundamental conditions which make the ontic possible. The ontological inquiry seeks the ontological conditions of possibility underlying any ontic expression or concrete being-in-the-world. One might conclude, therefore, that in claiming that his investigation is not ontological, Gilkey claims that the structures found are not essential and necessary to human being as such. Gilkey has attempted to address the situation of theological reflection, the structured context of presuppositions from which reflection arises today, and to found such theological reflection more solidly in light of the acute challenge of secularism and the challenge of the radical theologians. To do this, he has entered into the presuppositional base of reflection. It is precisely to such a base that this discussion must turn, but in the light of the former distinction between the ontic and the ontological.

It is generally agreed that reflection, as situated, emerges out of the concrete context of lived experience and, in some way, springs from an already understood stance toward the problematics or matter to be reflected upon. One might say that the issue to be interpreted is already understood, so that the thinker must, in an implicit manner, already understand what the thinking is attempting to explicate. This formulation of the situation of reflection indicates the circularity in such reflection: the thinker must already implicitly understand what he is attempting to understand.

That which is contained in the pre-understanding can be distinguished into that which is already understood or presupposed in a narrow sense and that which is already understood or presupposed in a broad sense. On the one hand, in the narrow sense, the ontic level of such presuppositional understanding simply focuses on the dimensions of the concrete entity's being-in-the-world which are presupposed for the raising of such questions. Reflection on this, for instance, would look for the concrete conditions of human existence and for the cultural elements involved in such a pre-understanding, if the attempt is made to explicate the foundational conditions from which such reflection emerges. In the case of theological reflection today, such an endeavor might well require that the present situation and ferment of theological activity be explicated, that any particular question be related to it, and that it then be related to the broader context of being-in-the-world of contemporary living. This, to a large extent, is the initial focus of the present investigation as it aims to limit to the ontic dimension what should not be considered ontological.

There is, however, a broader and more profound dimension of the presuppositional base of pre-understanding. The ontological dimensions of being-in-the-world enter radically into any inquiry, especially the temporal aspects of the ontological conditions as essential and necessary structures of existence presupposed as the foundation making possible any inquiry and shedding light on the implicit foundations from which the explication emerges. It is extremely important that this initial place be guaranteed without prejudice. It is not the purpose of the present study to investigate this level explicitly, but rather to ferret out certain aspects of existence and to prevent them from being attributed to the level of ontological foundation in foundational reflection. Consequently, a certain limitation of the ontological aspect in the presuppositional base of theological inquiry is the major concern of the present strictly philosophical reflection. This reflection attempts to reach certain elements of the presuppositional base and to explicate them in order to avoid claiming as essential and necessary to human existence a dimension which, although so claimed in many theological circles today by means of descriptive interpretation of phenomenological method, cannot stand up under the test of returning to the focal point and analyzing the truth of the foundations. It can be seen, then, that this presuppositional situation enters this study at both levels: first, at the level of explicating the concrete context of present day reflection which demands that the situation of pre-understanding be explicated to a limited extent as the context from which reflection emerges; second, in going beyond this level of the ontic to the ontological dimensions of human existence, at which level nothing which is not essential and necessary to human existence can be considered conditions of possibility for the being-in-the-world of human existence. It is precisely on this latter level that this study seeks to correct what has been implicitly considered a necessary dimension of existence. The limited aspects of the present presuppositional situation must be considered briefly.

It is not the contention of this study that reflection can emerge without presuppositions. In attempting to decipher and explicate presuppositions, especially those relevant to and influencing the fundamental orientation, content and method of reflection, both their ontic and ontological aspects, the present reflection attempts to highlight aspects of the ontic situation insofar as they comprise beliefs, values or generally accepted principles

which constitute our situation as the basis for reflection—
and, as in this case, especially for reflection on the religious. Thus, the situation will be approached with the
limited interest of finding and examining some essentially
determinative aspects of the contemporary situation influencing contemporary religious thought. In this endeavor, it will be helpful to clarify some aspects of the
contemporary backdrop or worldview in contrast to the
modern worldview, in explicating the presuppositional
base, inclusive of the options mentioned above.

The modern and contemporary contexts or worldviews
can be distinguished since their implicit frameworks are
different. These worldviews, although only implicitly operative in most reflection, can be explicated in such a way as to
indicate what must be understood for the adequate grasp
of the structure of contemporary pre-understanding. Further, it must be noted that the backdrop can be operative
on the level of abstract categorical reflection, as well as, at
least implicitly, on the lived level. As a matter of fact, the
more dominant aspects of a worldview, developed as the
result of second level reflective activity, usually become
implicitly operative on the lived level.

The contemporary worldview results and emerges from
the demise of the absolute, theoretical claims of modern
philosophy, and the concomitant return to lived experience as the source of and the court of appeal for knowledge. In the contemporary worldview, the absolute
acceptance of the content and product of a sophisticated
second level scientific reflection as the starting point and
framework of reflection becomes no longer the presuppositional requirement for reflection. Consequently, the contemporary worldview is the result of the rejection of claims
essential to the modern view: the claim of absolute ultimate categories in knowledge, the claim of absolute perspective, and the claim for approaching experience with
second-level content projected onto the basic level prior to
investigating philosophically its source. This last claim

reflects a philosophy springing from a naive and archaic view of science and of scientific method, a failure to reinterpret scientific method in the light of contemporary developments in science which reject reductionism, or a failure to appropriate some elements of a new method such as phenomenology, which corrects the claims of the modern view of science. The breakdown of these claims and the appeal to the things themselves of lived experience marks phenomenology's way of recasting the framework on the reflective level.

It is precisely in such a recasting of the worldview that many of the contemporary issues in theology have emerged, for in such a recasting, meanings and the knowledge to which they give rise are relative to the situation of the knowing community. Reality is grasped only through such meaning structures. Access to the transcendent as an unconditioned and absolute is admittedly limited, if not eliminated entirely, and the method, especially one such as phenomenology precisely as descriptive, must admit its limits. Therefore, the challenge to theological reflection as it emerges from the contemporary culture and reflection is intrinsic to the constitution of the contemporary world— or, in other terms, is intrinsic to the constitutive presuppositional totality. It is precisely to one aspect of such a challenge that the discussion shall now turn.

Langdon Gilkey contends that it is not viable to attempt theological reflection today without dealing in some way with the challenge of secularism. He says that: "To me, therefore, any current theology, Continental, English, or American, that does not recognize and seek reflectively to deal with this presence of secularity, of doubt, of skepticism, and so of a sense of the meaninglessness of religious language inside the Church as well as outside, and so inside the theologian and believer, is as far irrelevant to our present situation."[7] Characterizing the present world-

---

7. Gilkey, p. 10.

view as secular, he states further: "We are asking whether for our age religious belief itself, and with it metaphysical speculation, are possibilities at all, and therefore whether there is any way at all by which modern man can transcend the confinements of the secularist worldview."[8] In relating contemporary theological or philosophical reflection to the contemporary understanding of itself, which he calls *Geist*, Gilkey goes on to say: "Philosophical and theological methods, as does all human thinking, exist in the *historical* dimension and so are relative to the *Geist* of their age."[9]

The nature of the challenge of secularism, to a large extent, has become entangled in ambiguities and perhaps some equivocations. First and foremost, the impass to theology results in the at least implicit denial of the supernatural, of the ultimate transcendent, of the absolute, of the ultimate ground or order for human experience. Further equivocation results in the manifold sense of the term "transcendent," especially within the phenomenological tradition. Several issues are involved in this whole confusion. First of all, should the focus on the secular, even by the convinced secularist, be considered essentially devoid of ultimacy or of the religious dimensions of existence? Further, does all reflection in a contemporary worldview require secularism as the presuppositional context? Is it possible that this is only one way to obtain a neutral structural dimension of existence, accessible to another accidental way of being-in-the-world in a concrete way with a different presuppositional situation, and based on the will to believe or the fundamental option? The question is how to philosophize or theologize adequately from this contemporary backdrop in such a way as to explicate the presuppositional base from which reflection springs.

The point is that we must do justice to the whole situation of contemporary presuppositions, if we are to account

---

8. Gilkey, p. 20.
9. Gilkey, p. 190.

for the hermeneutical situation in an adequate reflection: from a base that can encompass both secularism and religious belief as not necessarily by presupposition mutually exclusive, and certainly not with the assumption that secularism or its opposite is the only and essential dimension of the contemporary worldview. So the qualification of the challenge from secularism has gone in two directions: first, in the directions of precluding the possibility of secularism being reconciled by some secularists with a religious attitude, and in not identifying the secularism with a negative thing, completing a dichotomy between the secular and the religious and thus excluding the position of Dewey; second, it has gone in the direction of the necessity of not identifying the contemporary worldview exclusively with secularism, especially in its narrow sense.

Recent efforts in foundational theology have focused on the meaningfulness of religious discourse rather than first and foremost on God or reality apprehensions. Further, the tendency has been to deal with the validity of theology in terms of the concrete tradition from which it springs and in which it is rooted.[10] Thus, the concrete community and its tradition become basic. This insight should not be overlooked, especially in terms of the overall presuppositional situation. Nevertheless, in the attempt to philosophically explicate the radical foundations of theology, this is not enough. Within reflection, several levels of option can be distinguished: that of the explicit denominational faith commitment concretely expressed in a particular denomination in its concrete situation and with its own tradition; second, that of the faith of the theist or atheist, more basic than the first option mentioned and presupposed by it; and finally, the structural dimension as the foundation of all these levels of options. Now inevitably, the question must be posed as to whether phenomenological theology in general, including that of Gilkey, has not

10. Farley, *Ecclesial Man*.

tended to presuppose in some way the validity of its own foundations within an option, and even with an implicit metaphyics, without sufficient rational reflective scrutiny.

Theologians certainly cannot be reproached for admitting their faith presupposition, commitment or option within which they begin reflection; but to claim philosophically radical foundation for such reflection demands philosophical adequacy. Hence, this project does not aim to destroy or even to question reflection beginning within options of secularism, of theism or, more specifically, of Christian or Hebrew commitments. Rather, it aims to seek philosophically the foundation for such reflections, whatever the weakness, strengths, or presuppositional strata of such a foundation might be.

Phenomenology has been employed on various levels as a method for radicalizing theology. Theological reflection can be brought to a radical level within particular religious denominations by the use of a phenomenology which attempts to explicate the experience underlying that tradition. These uses give rise to a pluralism in the theologies employing phenomenology due to the variations from one tradition to another. Further, such a use of phenomenology can be brought to a deeper level by investigating the overall religious experience which underlies any particular religious tradition. In this employment, it might be seen to uncover the essential aspects and dimensions of this type of experience and existence, that which underlies all religious traditions within the fundamental option of God belief. Finally, the use of the phenomenological method can be brought to explicate the essentially religious dimensions of existence, going deeper than the above analysis—laying bare the religious dimensions of existence without the prejudice of beginning within the presupposition that a God belief is necessary to existence for religious belief, experience or existence.

It is the contention of the present study that in order to radicalize philosophically the phenomenological approach as foundational to theological reflection, this last level of analysis is necessary, not to the theological project strictly as theological, but for philosophical adequacy. Thus, this reflection requires philosophically an investigation which undercuts the prejudice of a particular tradition and discloses the foundational aspects of experience and existence which are presupposed in such theological reflections. A consideration of radicalizing phenomenological theology, via some recent efforts in that direction, will explicate the direction and contours of such a project for today.

The seminal works in philosophical theology by such authors as Langdon Gilkey, Edward Farley and David Tracy[11] indicate a wide range for the possible use of phenomenology by theology. However, such theological treatments do not delineate a sufficiently radical philosophical level. Such a level is not necessarily the achievement of theology as such, but is demanded if that theology is to reach, by means of a descriptive interpretation, the radical presuppositional level of prereflective existence. This study has attempted to show that phenomenological theology reveals the radical structural level of lived experience in a philosophically adequate manner if it employs a phenomenology of religious experience to explicate the openness of existence. A phenomenology of religious experience, explicating the foundational level of openness of experience and existence within the strict limits of phenomenological method, radicalizes the phenomenology in theology, yet, at the same time, imposes serious limits on this descriptive level, as shall be seen.

Such a phenomenological analysis, delving into the fundamental level of existence as the root and foundation of religious experience *below* the subject-object disjunction, shows the fundamental openness at the heart of human

---

11. David Tracy, *Blessed Rage for Order: The New Pluralism*, (New York, The Seabury Press, 1975). Langdon Gilkey, *Naming the Whirlwind*. Edward Farley, *Ecclesial Man*.

existence as the foundation of *all* experience, even of religious experience. However, it becomes clear that, for such a phenomenological reflection on this foundational level, the structures of existence are neutral to God belief or God non belief. Religious beliefs, practices and intepretations exist within an option: i.e., the option for God belief, in contrast to the option against God belief, which also contains the religious aspect of experience as essential. At this foundational level of the existential openness of man's being-in-the-world, the nature of the root of knowledge and the fundamental dimensions of being can be descriptively interpreted without presupposition of theism or atheism reigning supreme at the outset. Further, the limits of this level, especially in relation to the realm of the presuppositions with which we begin philosophy, can be made thematic, but in relation to the nature and the claims of religious experience.

A phenomenology of religious experience separates the essential structures of religious existence from the dimensions of religious experience not essential to existence. Although some such dimensions of religious experience may indeed be essential to a particular type of religious experience within a particular option, this does not necessitate their being essential to religious *existence* as such. Any essential structure of religious existence, as the presupposed eidetic structure of religious experience, gives rise to an enigma: while the existential and presupposed foundation of belief in the Sacred is the ground of all theological and philosophical reflection, this same foundation is not included in the essential structures within existence—at least, it does not emerge as such within a phenomenology of existence achieved by focusing first on religious experience. What this means is that such a phenomenology of religious experience demands the liberation of the interpretation of the bond of human being to being, in being-in-the-world, from even a presuppositional tie to the Sacred as necessarily involving an absolute transcendent order. Such an analysis must allow for the interpretation of this bond to the Sacred even as absolute, as a possibility, but not as an eidetic aspect of existence, thus leaving room for the insightful contributions of Dewey and Sartre, and for the justification of either position in some way at a different level of reflection. It therefore requires that the same existential structure be essential to the atheistic life as well as to the theistic life. Thus, the essential and neutral structures of existence have emerged as central to existence whether it be ontically expressed as theistic or as atheistic. The Gordian knot of this paradox is intertwined with the realization that the whole person— the volitional and passional dimensions of existence included—on the presuppositional level, are at the root of *either* belief, even though there is not apodictic evidence justifying such a belief before it is accepted. However, that does not preclude reflection making sense out of such a commitment, in the context of the whole of life and the whole of reality, and explicitly confirming the position after the presuppositional strata are reflectively brought to light.

It is precisely in this context of the essential structures of experience and existence accessible to phenomenological analysis of lived experience that the use of phenomenology in the theologies of Langdon Gilkey, Edward Farley and David Tracy emerge as problematical. It is to their phenomenological theologies that the discussion will briefly turn in order to apply the conclusions reached in the preceding discussion concerning phenomenology of religious experience to the fundamental theses of Gilkey, Farley and Tracy. Gilkey's thesis shall be the first considered, since the application is more apparent and explicit. The same points apply equally to the others, rendering it unnecessary to treat them extensively.

While Gilkey's analysis has explicitly and honestly employed phenomenology, admitting the assumption and presupposition of the belief in the Sacred as the ultimate and unconditioned, his usage has not done full service to phenomenology in dealing with the essential structures of experience and existence in relation to the Sacred as the ultimate and unconditioned. Once a phenomenology of the structures of experience is undertaken, the structures must speak for themselves. It is precisely here that the use of phenomenology in the theology of Gilkey is problematical, for a phenomenological descriptive interpretation only uncovers the structures of experience that contain a belief in an order, coherence or ultimacy which are neutral to the metaphysical status which Gilkey gives to them. Such phenomenology, precisely as an eidetics of existence, does not include elements of Gilkey's presupposition within the eidetic dimensions of existence, since these elements are not essential to the religious aspect of existence. Yet he at least implicitly makes them eidetic. The phenomenology of religious experience, therefore, leads to a phenomenology of the religious in existence, with the result that the implicit metaphysical elements of Gilkey's presupposed faith must be excluded from an eidetics of existence.

To the extent that Gilkey's analysis in *Naming the Whirlwind* uncovers and discloses a radical faith, it has certainly not distorted that level of experience and of existence, as this study has tried to establish. Yet, presupposing the Sacred to include an ultimate order as an assumption feeding such a phenomenology, which, in turn, feeds and grounds theological discourse, is a failure to allow phenomenology to truly serve theologians in the most radical way possible.[12] Although it is not difficult to disclose a faith

---

12. Gilkey, p. 260; especially the following text: "A secular prolegomenon to theology, therefore, is one which begins in our ordinary experience of being in the world and elicits hermeneutically the meaning for religious language and its symbolic forms latent within that experience. What it seeks to uncover there are those aspects of daily experience which the secular mood has overlooked and consequently has not thematized or made explicit in the symbolic forms of its self-understanding. For as we have argued, there are levels latent in secular life of which our age is undoubtedly aware but about which it is unable to speak or to think intelligibly. These elements are the dimension of ultimacy presupposed

at the heart of the secularist worldview, [13] it cannot be so easily restricted to a faith in the Sacred necessarily interpreted in Gilkey's way, but, rather must remain true to the strict neutrality of phenomenological method.

Although Gilkey's attempt to make room for and employ a phenomenology which has both outgrown the narrow view of a phenomenology of consciousness and which has turned to the *Lebenswelt* is to be applauded, his polarization of such a phenomenology against an eidetic phenomenology is a misunderstanding of phenomenology. For phenomenology, *precisely as eidetic*, delves into the structural dimensions of experience in being-in-the-world. It is the contention of this study that such a phenomenology will find within the structure of experience or of existence an orientation to ultimacy. However, it is beyond phenomenological method to deal with the specific character of the object as requiring theism. Consequently, only the neutrality of eidetic phenomenology with regard to the ultimate is added to Gilkey's use of phenomenology and its findings. Although he is persistent in admitting that the Sacred as ultimate order is assumed, he makes no allowance for the other alternative and consequently falls into the one option and its presupposed but implicit metaphysics, therefore not attaining an adequate *philosophical* foundation for phenomenological theology. It is his phenomenological theology which is qualified as requiring a further foundation. Nevertheless, it must be admitted, Gilkey sometimes seems to speak precisely within those limits.

The philosophical theologies of Farley and Tracy seem similarly to fit within the theistic option and its presup-

---

in all our interaction with the relative world and the presence of ambiguity within our freedom and our creativity, of the demonic and the despairing in life as well as the joyful, with both of which secular experience is suffused. In these terms, the symbols of our theological tradition may come alive in a secular age, and the possibility of a meaningful discourse about God in our time be established."

13. Gilkey, pp. xii and ff.

posed but implicit metaphysics, which they both admit. This can be briefly indicated without investigating the developments of their respective theses.

Farley's treatment of ecclesial man attempts to delve into a radical level but in an entirely different manner and in a different context than that of Gilkey, although he treats themes similar to Gilkey's as a correlation to the development of his basic theme. He focuses on the transcendental foundation of communal faith existence, explicating the structures, essence or kernel of the lived world of a faith community, beginning with a particular faith community, phenomenologically analyzing it for its implicit meaning, and bringing to light its prereflective foundation.[14] As a viable phenomenological enterprise, it is not exclusive of Gilkey's level of consideration, nor does it claim to be so. Nevertheless, one must not be oblivious to the validity of his claim that faith in its structure is communal, integrating this thesis with the phenomenological notion of intersubjectivity. Thus, in moving from Gilkey to Farley and then to the most radical foundational level of faith prescinding from any metaphysical claim about the status of the ultimate in the faith in the Sacred, the explicit account of intersubjectivity on this level must be taken into account. Nevertheless, Farley's phenomenological treatment of ecclesial man in the context of the lived world requires the corrective qualification concerning the essential dimensions of the religious existence as derived from a phenomenology of religious experience, as has been seen.

Tracy's revisionist model, perhaps the most broad incorporation of phenomenology in theology among the three authors mentioned, must be said to operate within the same option as the other two: within a certain presupposed faith including an implicit metaphysical aspect. This is manifest in his attempt to explicate the implicit religious orientation within the scientific attitude, and the implicit

---

14. Gilkey, pp. xii and ff.

scientific in the religious attitude. This treatment, in his context of fundamental Christian theology as philosophical reflection on the meanings in common human experience and language and on the meanings in Christian fact,[15] uses phenomenology and hermeneutics to bring to light both poles mentioned in this description of theology. Phenomenology is employed to disclose the religious dimension of common human experience, but in a way which presupposes an interpretation of the faith option which has already been made.[16] Again, it must be said, this is not an invalid enterprise or use of phenomenology by theology, but it lacks radical foundation in its interpretation of that faith in relation to the meaning and structures of common human existence. It is thus subject to the qualification and critical remarks already addressed to the positions of Gilkey and Farley.

Gilkey's view of the presuppositional level of faith in the Sacred, Farley's view of the intersubjective and prereflective faith, and Tracy's view of the religious dimension of common human experience and existence, all *ignore the possibility*, latent within such an existential faith, of neutrality in the ultimacy of the object of faith. This study suggests a radical foundational aspect of faith lacking in the uses of phenomenology in these three theologies. While this study does not destroy or even qualify that theological manner of interpretation, it attempts to delve deeper, in a *strictly philosophical way*, to the further possibility latent in that presupposed level of faith, uncovering further and more explicitly an essential structure latent in and neutral to the alternative options. Such an ultimate is open to being interpreted as God or as an ideal, or in some other fashion, so that this radical level of faith inherent in existence is not predetermined as an ultimate absolute behind and other than what appears. The philosophizing

15. Tracy, *Blessed Rage for Order*, pp. 43 ff. and p. 91.
16. Tracy, p. 43.

"before God" and not about God is not invalidated but, rather, is given further philosophically explicated ground. That limitation gives room for an alternate option, opens theoretical and faith commitments to explicit admissions of the need and the place for tolerance of alternate beliefs, and, at once, admits the full limit of phenomenology wedded to theology as descriptive method. At the same time, it suggests to the theologian-philosopher the further need to justify or rationally account for the content of his presuppositional faith option in a way that phenomenology as such cannot do.

A radical philosophy is not the achievement of theology as such, but is necessary if that theology claims complete radicalization, and if it attempts to use phenomenology to get at the radical presuppositional level of prereflective existence. It has been the thesis of this study that to *philosophically* radicalize the phenomenological analysis of existence within theological reflection, the radical structural level of existence must at some point be attained as the ultimate presuppositional base, and that such a philosophically foundational project of reflection requires a focus on existence as the presuppositional context of the commitments from which reflection emerges. Gilkey, Farley and Tracy, therefore, have not achieved a sufficiently radical philosophical level in their respective treatments of religious existence.

Phenomenology, within the limits of descriptive interpretations, cannot so determine the object of religious experience. It can be found within a strictly philosophical inquiry that the openness of existence is eidetically neutral to the specific content of the object side of religious experience. However, even theologians reflecting within a specific faith option are free to take up this analysis for their own use, provided they have not already closed that door by means of a descriptive phenomenology. If, however, they are to make the claim that to be human is to have chosen this option, including certain absolute and unconditioned aspects of the object involved in that response, without admitting to themselves the neutrality of the structural aspect of existence, then the dynamics and the basis of that option must be examined. For it is one thing to attempt to account for one's own position within an option and quite another to claim that this is the only option possible to humans if they are existing humanly. The theologians mentioned seem to claim more than the former. Yet, this attempt to philosophically radicalize phenomenological theology does not substantially alter their descriptive accounts of Christian existence but, rather, puts it in a clear philosophical focus.

CHAPTER FOUR

Religious Existence and Existential Phenomenology

This chapter must pursue further the consequences of the conclusions of the preceding investigations, especially relevant to the neutrality of presuppositional existence regarding any religious object. It is here that the move from religious convictions, retained within a specific option, to a philosophical analysis of human existence often allows a subtle religious presupposition to remain intact. To orient this study of human existence precisely as religious yet neutral to God belief and to an adherence to the Sacred on the ontic level, a brief discussion of contemporary humanism, inclusive of a philosophically acceptable view of the religious in existence, will prove foundational. Such a reflection on a viable contemporary humanism ties together the themes of the preceding investigations, while, at once, laying the foundation for a critique of a view of human existence which pervades the use of phenomenology in theology today, and the treatments of the ontic relation to the Sacred usually central to such use of phenomenology. The purpose of this chapter, then, is to explicate more adequately the foundational character of human existence within an existential phenomenology as a pervasively contemporary philosophy.

THE SENSE OF CONTEMPORARY HUMANISM[1]

Humanism in a certain sense has become all things to all people. For humanism—extolling the dignity and value of

1. The following pages on "The Sense of Contemporary Humanism"

humankind as such and emphasizing the interest, uniqueness and limit of humans—has become broad enough to include Sartre's atheistic existentialism, the role of human beings in the emergence of truth according to Heidegger, and the possibility of a religious humanism. Since such disparate philosophies have espoused and have been embraced by an ever-widening sense of humanism, it is timely to broach again this perhaps tired and retired question about the sense of humanism in order to ferret out and rejuvenate its precise and unified sense for today, and its foundational character in relation to religious existence.

The ensuing discussion will attempt to restore to human existence (humanism) a philosophical and contemporary sense which is cognizant of the contemporary interpretation of the modern philosophy of human limits, of the central role of freedom in human existence, and of the unique being of humans in the revelation of being, all within the context of the possibility of a foundation for religious humanism. Such a philosophical consideration is possible only on the basis of the rejection of the modern philosophical framework which is forced into reductionism or dualism due to its understanding of the place of humans in nature. In addition, the question of whether there is such a thing as religious humanism which does not jeopardize the dignity of the human person must be confronted.

In an attempt to derive a unified sense of contemporary humanism, it is important to consider the contrast between the modern and the contemporary philosophic frameworks dealt with briefly in the last chapter. Contemporary philosophy, arising out of the ashes of the collapsed claims of modern philosophy as the philosophical basis of modern science, and confronting the need for an entirely different philosophical base for a new science, places humankind in a unique but not overplayed role in philosophy. In the

---

were read at the Segundo Congreso Mundial De Filosofia Christiana in Monterey, N.L., Mexico, in 1986, and printed in the proceedings.

contemporary worldview, the absolute acceptance of the content and product of a sophisticated second-level scientific reflection as its starting point and framework becomes no longer the presuppositional requirement for reflection. As mentioned in the preceding chapter, the contemporary worldview is the result of the rejection of essential elements of the modern view: the claims of an absolute perspective, the understanding of nature as mechanistic, and the distortion of experience by projecting second-level content onto the basic experiential level. These claims, sometimes still philosophically operative today, reflect a philosophy springing from a naive and archaic view of science and scientific method, a failure to reinterpret scientific method in the light of contemporary developments in science which demonstrate a broader view of scientific method and which rejects reductionism. The breakdown of these claims and the appeal to the things themselves of lived experience marks phenomenology's way of recasting the framework on the reflective level.

Fundamentally, the alternatives of reductionism or dualism within the philosophy embracing mechanism are replaced by a philosophy which grasps a harmony and richness in the relation between nature and humans, expressing an entirely different philosophy for today. For such a contemporary philosophy, knowledge is brought back to earth and seen to be rooted in the richness of lived experience. The foundational level of meaning and its origin can be interpreted from the epistemic point of view, revealing the central role of human existence in the origin of meaning. Investigating this originary level reveals that human existence as intentional is constitutive of meaning, that the quasi-organic relation between the perceiver and the world is the lived context of the emergence of meanings and is the theatre of action, that there is receptivity and activity central to prereflective intentional experience at the originary level of meaning.

This contemporary vision reveals a harmony between

nature and the human, overcoming the modern antinomy between freedom and nature or necessity by means of an enriched nature in humans and humans in nature.[2] Lived nature, which includes the weddedness of humans to nature both within and outside the human, the lived body, and lived existence reveal a freedom in being-in-the-world which does not separate humans from the lived world and lived nature but, rather, bespeaks a unity of existing humans with the world and within themselves. It is to the philosophies of existence as one expression of, and embodiment by, humanism that the discussion will now turn

---

2. For instance, Paul Ricoeur's adjustment in the Kantian doctrine on the antinomy between nature and freedom can be summarized this way: first, sensibility must be capable of a relation to willing as a motive for decision which *inclines without compelling*; second, a rational principle must be capable of touching me in a way analogous to that of sensible goods. Indeed, for Kant, respect is a *sui generis* feeling of subordination of the will to a law without any other intermediary influence on sensibility, so that, in respecting its own rationality, the will receives nothing, but spontaneously produces the feeling of respect in itself, thereby restoring sovereignty to reason. [Paul Ricoeur, *Freedom and Nature: The Voluntary and the Involuntary*, translated by Erazim Kohak (Evanston: Northwestern University Press, 1966), p. 131.] Ricoeur, in another place, observes: "Respect, as a practical feeling, posits a limit to my ability to act," still close to the Kantian context of respecting humanity as an objective end, as an end which I should never act against. [Paul Ricoeur, *Husserl: An Analysis of His Phenomenology*, translated by Edward G. Ballard and Lester Embree (Evanston: Northwestern University Press, 1976), p. 199] In expanding the function and role of respect to parallel that of the transcendental imagination in the cognitive synthesis, Ricoeur also changes the role of duty from the strictly Kantian role. Rather, for him the relation between motive and project is far more inclusive if liberated from such a Kantian ethical a priori. In a way which entails the possibility of the person as bodily comportment, Ricoeur also considers desire to be a motive or a value and not a cause. Such spontaneities can incline without compelling the will and thus serve as a basis for decision without mitigating active freedom as human and receptive. To recast the Kantian relationship between freedom and necessity in phenomenological terms, Ricoeur speaks of the reciprocity between the voluntary and the involuntary. Given this experiential focus, he dispenses with the need to postulate freedom as a cause in the strictly Kantian sense. Indeed, for him the whole of the voluntary in all three of its moments must be receptive to the involuntary as already human and therefore as liberated from a causal language which is reductive of motive, powers of action, and life.

in order to make explicit a contemporary philosophical humanism.

An at least implicit humanism lies latent within contemporary philosophies of existence, all of which, one way or another, focus primarily on human existence in its totality and concreteness, with freedom at its core.[3] Paradoxically, none of the diverging existential senses of humanism miss the mark, since each focuses on something essential to a genuine contemporary humanism (although in some cases perhaps in exaggerated formulations). To support the stress on the central role of human freedom, even limited, is reminiscent of classical humanism. An extreme formulation of such humanism today is Sartre's claim that his existentialism is a humanism[4] in the sense that existence precedes the essence of humans, so that the chief human value is human freedom, from which all essential dimensions of human being emerge, thus putting freedom in a quasi-absolute role at the core of human existence.[5] Sartre, however, focuses on the negative dimensions of freedom as the human person's rejection of being in the fixed mode of en soi, and identifies human existence as being what it is

3. See: Patrick L. Bourgeois and Frank Schalow, "Freedom, Finitude, and Totality: Ricoeur and Heidegger," *Journal of the British Society for Phenomenology*, Vol. 18, No. 3, October 1987. The manner in which any contemporary philosophy resolves the Kantian antinomy between freedom and nature entails the relation between finitude and totality. Ricoeur and Heidegger, both relevant to the discussion of this chapter, can be seen to resolve the third antinomy within respective philosophical orientations which entail differing views of finitude and totality. More specifically, Ricoeur employs an extended sense of the Kantian limiting concept, primarily addressing the issues on a quasi-ethical level with a philosophy of the will. In contrast, Heidegger resolves the antinomy in a more radical way on the level of fundamental ontology, extending his own view of the ontological sense of finitude, hence cutting beneath Ricoeur's orientation and opposing certain points essential to his view of totality.

4. Jean-Paul Sartre, "Existentialism is a Humanism," in *Existentialism from Dostoevsky to Sartre*, edited by Walter Kaufmann (Cleveland, Ohio: The World Publishing Co., 1956), pp. 290 ff.

5. Jean-Paul Sartre, *Being and Nothingness*, translated by Hazel E. Barnes (New York: Washington Square Press, Inc. 1953), Introduction and Part Four, Chapter One.

not, and not being what it *is*.[6] Thus, the value and dignity of human existence, as free, rests in the uniqueness of its mode of being. It is precisely this which Heidegger wishes to correct, since Sartre's humanism, according to Heidegger, falls short of the real value and dignity of being as Dasein.[7] In this context, if the term humanism still has meaning today, it must include the process of unconcealing the meaning and truth of being, which is occasioned by Dasein as the "shepherd of being."[8]

Heidegger's interpretation of humanism may grant a deeper significance for the possibility of humanism today, and, at once, allow for the possibility of a religious reinterpretation, although this is perhaps not Heidegger's intent. In his now famous treatment of humanism, Heidegger has given some insight to the role of humans in an ontology which goes beyond the traditional view of metaphysics. The relation between human being and being, or the way of being of humans as Dasein and being, puts the metaphysical questions of old into a new context, so that it is not merely entities which are dealt with, but rather the revealing of the being process as it comes to thought. The primary and originary transcendence, which belongs to human being and which is expressed as being-in-the-world, is more fundamental than the relations among entities.[9] This decentering of humans or of the being of humans in favor of a primacy of being does not destroy humanism, but puts the truth of being in the important central focal place. Yet being-in-the-world and humanism fit together. For to do justice to the role of humans in

---

6. Sartre, *Being and Nothingness*, p. lxxviii.

7. Martin Heidegger, "Letter on Humanism" in *Basic Writings*, edited by David F. Krell (New York: Harper and Row, 1977), pp. 208 ff.

8. Heidegger, pp. 208 ff.

9. This statement implicitly refers to the relation between intentionality and transcendence. This correlation is important enough for a special treatment later in this chapter particularly since the manner in which their relation is interpreted greatly influences the view of human existence, as shall be seen.

general, as an expression of humanism—the fundamentally ontological orientation toward human existence, even though it is only a beginning of ontology attempting to delve into the sense of being and to unconceal being as it reveals itself—shows that existence as the way of being of Dasein is central to the being process. This, however, is not a metaphysics of humans as such, but rather an ontology of Dasein. As such, it must be seen that the focus is not upon entities as such, but rather upon being and the place of Dasein. This place humbles Dasein: " 'Humanism' now means, in case we decide to retain the word, that the essence of man is essential for the truth of being, specifically in such a way that the word does not pertain to man simply as such."[10] In marked contrast to this replacing of humans, yet, at once, appropriating the humble role of Dasein in the truth of being, is another philosophy emerging out of the backdrop of existential philosophy. A rejuvenated philosophy of limits, together with an ontology of Dasein and an ontology of symbols, emerges as a possible philosophic basis for a revamped humanism.

It is precisely in this context that Paul Ricoeur sees humanism as a philosophy of limits.[11] A philosophy of limits can be taken in several senses. First of all, a philosophy of limits deals with the Kantian context of the limit idea, which is not an object of experience and which is not constitutive of knowledge, but which can serve a regulative role in directing reason to the total and to completion regarding an unconditioned. In the present context, however, the philosophy of limits dwells on the limits which are essential to philosophical anthropology. Limit is the context of such a philosophy which reflects on the different aspects of human being. The quest for the total and the complete in the line of reason is limited. As Ricoeur says:

---

10. Heidegger, "Letter on Humanism," p. 224.

11. Paul Ricoeur, "What Does Humanism Mean?", in *Political and Social Essays*, edited by David Stewart and Joseph Bien (Athens, Ohio: Ohio University Press, 1974), esp. pp. 85–87.

"I think everything and I demand everything, but I am never able to know it. Kant only applied to cosmology his golden rule of the limiting function of the concept of the thing-in-itself. But it is necessary to apply to the totality of history this *limiting* role of the ideal of its total meaning and to raise it up against all pretensions that would say what this total meaning is. That is the fundamental principle of the thesis according to which the efficaciousness of the man of culture, and its corollary in a liberal politics of culture, is the object of belief and not of knowledge."[12] For Ricoeur, the remembrance of death indicated in the very name of the human introduces the reference to a limit at the very heart of the affirmation of humans as such. "When faced with the pretension of absolute knowledge, humanism is therefore the indication of an 'only': we are only men."[13] It is to the foundational level of the existential openness of human being-in-the-world that the discussion will briefly turn in order to reveal the indirect access to the Sacred within limit expressions, and to uncover the essence of a humanism as contemporary and as foundation for a religious humanism.

As seen already,[14] the analysis of human existence can be limited in its focus to the ontic aspects in contrast to the ontological aspects. Such ontic analysis, focusing upon the entity simply as an entity, can interpret everyday living in a concrete world with its presuppositions, structures and habits, or it can include any or all of many worlds, for instance, the workaday world, or the religious world within a belief or commitment, or a particular political world, etc. These various worlds and commitments of everyday concrete existence can come under scrutiny and

---

12. Ricoeur, "What Does Humanism Mean?", p. 86.
13. Ricoeur, "What Does Humanism Mean?", p. 86.
14. The transition from an ontic to an ontological analysis has been treated in Chapter Three, but is important enough to warrant a brief mention here as preliminary to the development of ontological aspects of existence.

analysis without their ontological conditions being revealed as such, and without the analysis becoming ontological. This is the claim made by philosophical theology
today,[15] that this analysis of the Sacred in relation to
existence is not ontological, and that the Sacred in the life
of the religious person and the Sacred or unconditioned in
the implicit aspects of the lived experience of the secularist
are not ontological, but rather ontic, as shall be seen.

In order for such an inquiry to become ontological, it
must go beyond the ontic level and penetrate to the fundamental conditions which make the ontic possible. The
ontological inquiry seeks the ontological conditions of possibility underlying any ontic expression or concrete being-
in-the-world. Thus, if this investigation is not ontological,
then the structures found are not essential and necessary
to human being as such. This means that a phenomenology of religious existence, as descriptive interpretation,
demands the liberation of the interpretation of the bond
between human existence and being, in being-in-the-
world, from even a presuppositional tie to the Sacred as
necessarily involving an absolute transcendent order. Such
an analysis must allow for the interpretation of this bond to
the Sacred as a *possibility*, but not as a necessary and eidetic
aspect of existence, thereby indicating explicitly the place
for the foundation of a religious humanism.

Although not an ontological dimension of existence, the
orientation to the Sacred as ontic belongs to the structure
of a concrete way of being-in-the-world, and can possibly
be considered within a reinterpretation of the meaning and
being of truth as its ontological condition of possibility.
The Sacred is accessible to reflection and to experience
through the indirect language of symbols. The symbols
and symbolic structure in general provide the means for
overcoming the limitations of experience and of the relation to being revealed in experience, existence and lan-

---

15. See Gilkey, *Naming the Whirlwind*, pp. 336, 413.

guage, to reach what can only be thought but which cannot be known. The symbols of the Sacred, then, are correlated to reason striving to think the unconditioned, but with a limitation to the regulative function of indirect expressions and limit experience, thereby avoiding the overclaim of knowledge of absolutes and of absolute knowledge.

This limit function is still relevant even in the contemporary philosophy which denies the dichotomy between the phenomenon and noumenon. The limit is manifest in experience, language and concept, and in the preconceptual comprehension of being. The total is not given exhaustively, and the fullness of meaning is not encompassed completely, so that the revelation is ongoing and continuous. The indirect language par excellance is the symbol, with its semantic structure containing double meaning, a literal meaning which leads to a latent meaning. It is this symbolic structure which allows the symbol to give and to give rise to thought, and, at once, to reveal a certain truth of being. It is here that some contemporary theologians, reflecting from within their religious options, interpret the symbol's ultimate significance, evinced in various contexts, to be the Sacred. As such, this is the existential foundation and place for a religious and Christian appropriation of, and inclusion within, a contemporary humanism. Further, this humanism stands within the fullness and richness of a contemporary rendition of the relation between nature and the human, which, in turn, is included within a philosophy of limits. The hubris of a blind humanism is therefore overcome, and, at once, a foundation for a religious humanism is won.

This discussion of a philosophy of limits, limit concepts, limit experiences and expressions, and the neutral structures of existence brings us to the heart of a consideration which must be undertaken before investigating the implications of a humanistic view of existence in terms of the creative and central role of imagination in the production of images which go beyond experience, in response to the demand of reason. Another difficulty concerning human existence must be further clarified, since it is both central to this whole investigation and essential to the thinking of Paul Ricoeur, whose work has been appropriated in one way or another by most of the phenomenological theologians mentioned in the last chapter. A brief treatment and adjustment of this view of human existence will lay bare the foundation for a consideration of the role of the imagination in forming expressions for a dimension of existence and for limit expressions central to our discussion on the possibility of religious existence and experience.

THE INTEGRITY AND FALLENNESS OF HUMAN EXISTENCE

It was Ricoeur's initial interest in a philosophy of the will which drew his attention to the broader significance of hermeneutics in his later and more explicitly religious writings. Yet he has maintained an intense interest, from the beginning of his writings, in the religious, prephilosophical dimensions of existence. His philosophical writings on the religious generally take place within the presuppositional option of the Christian response and involve, on a radical level, a relation to the Sacred. It is within his options that he analyzes symbols, metaphorical contexts and their foundations.

Central to Ricoeur's philosophy of the will, to his philosophical anthropology, and to his religious philosophy is the correlation between human existence and Transcendence.[16] It must be noted that Transcendence takes on a certain absoluteness, and is more limited than the notion of transcendence in phenomenology as constitutive of all experience, existence and being-in-the-world. This Ricoeurean Transcendence as the Sacred in experience, although not called God or Absolute Being, is meant to depict that to

16. Patrick L. Bourgeois, *Extension of Ricoeur's Hermeneutic* (The Hague, Nijhoff, 1975), pp. 23–27, esp. pp. 26–27.

which religious existence is oriented. Ricoeur is explicit in the initial focus in Volume One of his philosophy of the will to bracket out both Transcendence and existence. He attempts to hold in focus the essential aspects of the human, underlying any accidental conditions of concrete existence on the ontic level, especially within the general problem of evil.

The ensuing discussion will show that Ricoeur's view of the existential locus of evil in the disproportionate synthesis between the finite and the infinite in humans is somewhat truncated. In marked contrast, Heidegger's view of the "essence" or way of being (*Wesen*) of humans as existence can be considered in terms of its underlying preconceptual comprehension of Being, but with special focus upon the existential structures of being-in-the-world in its fundamental unity and wholeness.[17] More specifically, for Heidegger there is no strong impulse to address the problem of evil nor a concern to identify a special philosophical locus within the existential structures of Dasein to account for evil. Hence, the following questions emerge: to what extent can Heidegger's view of existence as "Being-there" (Dasein) be instructive for recasting Ricoeur's view of existence as fallen? Is it necessary to consider human existence to be already fallen in the sense that the will, in its actual conditions, is enslaved? How do we then account for the existential possibility of basically good people who do not claim any regeneration or redemption, but simply manifest good will and goodness of will?

For Ricoeur, the eidetics of human willing yields an abstraction prescinding from the actual conditions of existence. According to the preface to *Fallible Man*,[18] it is the

---

17. For a full contrast between Ricoeur and Heidegger on the place of evil in human existence, see: Frank Schalow and Patrick L. Bourgeois, "The Integrity and Fallenness of Human Existence," *The Southern Journal of Philosophy*, Vol. 25, No. 1 (Spring 1987).

18. Paul Ricoeur, *Fallible Man*, trans. by Charles Kelbley (Chicago: Henry Regnery Company, 1965), p. xvi.

"undifferentiated keyboard" upon which is reverberated the various existences of humans, as innocent, fallen, and regenerated in redemption. The attempt to separate the eidetic from the existential dimensions establishes the merely accidental character of existence as fallen, avoiding the danger of ontologizing the fault in the human's existential constitution. It is precisely the tension and differences between the abstract human and existing human, or, in another context, between the eidetics of the will and the pure reflection on the existential structures of humans, which proves decisive for Ricoeur.

The fundamental limit placed on an eidetic level of reflection upon willing is obviously that inherent in any eidetic reflection. As such it will "bracket the fact and elaborate the sense,"[19] in the attempt to arrive at structures of willing, structures of the human, in pure reflection yielding essential dimensions. The first product of this abstraction and eidetic analysis of the voluntary and the involuntary is the reciprocity between them, taking their unity to be a Kantian limit concept.

As long as the task of an eidetics of the will is simply to articulate the meanings of the will and motives and desire, acting and ability to act, of consenting and necessity, the unity of the voluntary and the involuntary holds up. But as soon as the effort is made to elaborate an existential synthesis, "as soon as one tries to get closer to the concrete life of consciousness, to the existential development of an individual, the failure of the unity becomes manifest."[20] It is precisely the failure of the unity which throws into focus the notion of the Kantian regulative unity. Ricoeur, however, wishes to extend the use of regulative ideas beyond

---

19. Paul Ricoeur, *Freedom and Nature: The Voluntary and the Involuntary*, translated by Erazim Kohak (Evanston: Northwestern University Press, 1966), pp. 2–3.
20. Paul Ricoeur, "The Unity of the Voluntary and the Involuntary as a Limiting Idea, in *Readings in Existential Phenomenology*, edited by Nathaniel Lawrence and Daniel O'Connor (New Jersey: Prentice Hall, 1967) p. 105.

the Kantian foundation of scientific knowledge, proposing a human ideal, a meaning for human unity which is the idea of a motivated, incarnate, contingent freedom.[21] In contrast, Heidegger explicates the unity of Dasein in terms of care. Given Ricoeur's focus, it is not surprising that he should criticize Heidegger for too quickly arriving at such a unity. For Ricoeur, this unity can be deciphered from myths and stories in which its experiences are manifested, or it can be taken as a limit concept or as a task; but it must not be too quickly affirmed ontologically as the human's mode of being, identifying unity with an a priori structure which is already achieved rather than as a fight to be won.

Since the abstraction of the fault and of Transcendence are inseparable, one implying the other, the abstraction of Transcendence is also necessary.[22] The experience of fault and the mythical vision of innocence are closely linked with an affirmation of Transcendence. Transcendence is what liberates freedom from the fault. Humans live Transcendence as purification and deliverance of their freedom as salvation. The myth of innocence involves the beginning and the end, the genesis and the eschatology.

Such an abstraction is admittedly a limitation. It is only later, in the releasing of the abstraction, that the fuller understanding of humans and their structures can be grasped. However, the abstraction supplies the guiding themes and a limit for fundamental ontology. Without such a limit, there is danger of existential monism and of ontologizing accidental aspects of man's empirical existence. Thus Ricoeur, beginning with an eidetics, clears the way for a grasp of the Being of the human condition in

---

21. Ricoeur, "The Unity of the Voluntary and the Involuntary . . .," p. 107.

22. For clarity's sake, it is important to emphasize that Ricoeur alludes to "transcendence" in the narrow sense entailing man's affinity with God, while Heidegger identifies this phenomenon in order to clarify the ontological meaning of being-in-the-world. Though the different connotations Heidegger and Ricoeur assign to this term closely parallel the differences which have been revealed in their views on "falling," it would take us too far afield to develop this complementary problem.

fundamental ontology. This becomes clear from the fundamental principle yielded by this pure description, from the
polemical unity of the human as a regulative idea. It is this
study's contention that the ontology allowed for should be
slightly different from the one he envisions, demanding an
essential adjustment in his view of the locus of evil in the
existential structures of existence. It is to this existential
development that the discussion will now turn.

Ricoeur has made an important distinction at the outset
of his eidetics upholding the view that underlying the
variations of the empirical human and contingency, there
is an essential nature presupposed both by innocence and
fault, one which can be obtained through eidetic description. Thus, at the outset of his philosophy of the will, great
pains are taken not to put accidental characteristics on this
level of the essential structures of human willing.

Ricoeur wishes to turn to the symbols and myths as a
means of access to the accidental conditions of humans. It
is the eidetic dimensions, not the existential structures,
which underlie all three modes of concrete existence, as
their undifferentiated keyboard: the concrete existences of
the innocent, of the fallen, and of the regenerated. It has
been seen that in order to reach essential structures and
relationships of structures, abstraction from the concrete
and variable aspects is necessary. The descent from the
eidetic reflection on the abstract human to concrete reflection on the concrete human is a gradual one. The interme-
diate stage between them is the pure reflection of *Fallible
Man* which is concerned with the existential structures of
disproportion and synthesis. This synthesis is not merely
that of the objectivity of the object in the subjectivity of the
subject for strictly theoretical knowledge, as is the case for
Kant. For Ricoeur, it is fundamentally a question of the
unity of humans especially in the practical and affective
synthesis. He extends his perspective as broadly as possible to consider a global view of humans, taking the transcendental method as his guideline, rendering problematic

the human totality and extending the method, even on the object, to practical antinomies and their synthesis and then to the affective poles and synthesis. Following the transcendental guidance and beginning with the synthesis of the transcendental imagination, he progresses through the feeling of respect as the synthesis of character and happiness, and finally to the affective synthesis of life and logos. While the cognitive and, for the most part, the practical syntheses are thrown outward onto the object, the affective realm brings the synthesis into the interiority of the human, to what Ricoeur calls the heart (*thymos*). This synthesis marks the depth of human disproportion in feeling. It is the function of feeling first to accomplish a bond to things, to beings, to Being. This has been revealed by the unity of its intentionality and affection. The inner conflict of the self with the self is also revealed as presupposed for interiorizing the exterior conflicts in culture and in history.

It is perhaps at this point that it is possible to pause and criticize Ricoeur for remaining too Kantian in spite of his fundamental opposition to Kant's view of the place of evil in humans. In such a critique, what emerges is the view that the structures of human existence are, like the eidetic structures, equally foundational for innocent, fallen, and regenerated existence. It is precisely existence which is neutral to all of these, and the bracketing of fault, innocence, passion and Transcendence should be extended to and maintained within a pure reflection on existence. For existence is not only manifest as fallen, and the conditions which make evil will possible are equally the conditions which make good will possible. In this context it is necessary to turn to the place of radical evil adapted from Kant.

Ricoeur has disagreed with Kant's treatment of evil in human existence by denying that its place is only in the inclinations and by disavowing Kant's opposing sensibility to reason and to the a priori of moral order. For Ricoeur, the existential locus of evil is couched in the existential fallibility of humans, rooted in the disproportion in the synthesis between the infinite and the finite rather than in sensibility alone. This disproportion is expressed in the realms of the cognitive synthesis achieved by the transcendental imagination, the practical synthesis achieved by respect, and by the affective synthesis of the heart. Therefore the fragile synthesis leads to the downfall in concrete human existence in which the rational propensity for the total is sought in finite objects or objectifications, thus idolatizing why indirectly accessible as though it were an object of experience or a being.

This access through the indirect expressions of myth to a unity or to a limit concept leads to the difference between this abstract dimension of the human yielded by eidetic analysis, and the existential dimensions derived from a pure reflection upon the structures of existence yielding the locus of evil in existence.

The existential conditions of the possibility of fallenness, in the sense of the evil or hardened heart—or, in more Kantian terms, the evil of the maxim of the will—are the same existential conditions or structures of the good will, of seeking the highest good, and of regeneration to a new life. To consider fallenness accidental to the essential structures of willing may still be too Kantian for a contemporary philosophy, which should go the further step and consider fallenness as a possibility instead of as a necessity belonging to the existential structure of synthesis.

The attempt to develop an extended, more "neutral" sense of falling is precisely the adjustment operative in Heidegger's existential analytic. His approach incorporates falling within the essential structure of Dasein's Being, thereby relieving it of its purely accidental character. In almost an inverse manner, Ricoeur works from the premise that existence derives its significance from the accidental condition of humans as fallen. Inevitably, his analysis creates a gulf between the structures that define humans essentially and the concrete occurrence of the self. The very thrust of Heidegger's approach lies precisely in preventing this gulf from ever arising.

97

It seems, then, that Ricoeur should perhaps be more open to Heidegger's view of the existence of Dasein as the neutral conditions of the possibility of evil and of good. These can be maintained without compromising his philosophic conviction, different from that of Heidegger, of human existence as the synthesis of finite and infinite, and of the necessity to treat the ontic or existentiell level of existence more extensively and directly than Heidegger does, as shall be seen after a brief contrast between Ricoeur's and Sartre's treatments of the religious. Contrasting and integrating insights from Ricoeur and Sartre, each assuming different religious options as do James and Dewey, will serve to further clarify certain aspects of the religious existence and the necessity of admitting the neutrality of that level.

Sartre presents a somewhat paradoxical account of a preontological comprehension of God constitutive òf human existence. When Sartre's phenomenological ontology, and indeed, existential phenomenology in general, deepens and broadens the notion of intentionality, it goes to the prepredicative and prejudgmental level of origins and to the *lived world*. For Sartre, the being of the en soi as the mode of being of things and the transphenomenality of being emerged in the context of the prereflective intentionality which has transcendence as its constitutive structure. The emergence of the mode of pour soi, as the mode of being of humans, is correlated to the mode of en soi, within the foundational dimensions of being. Consequently, the two modes of being are intentionally correlated, so that human consciousness is constitutively transcendence and primordially involves a primacy of being and not a primacy of knowledge. For Sartre, the prereflective cogito is the primary and originary consciousness, foundation for all reflection, in terms of which he expresses this primacy of Being. He expresses its intentionality as follows:

All consciousness is consciousness of something. This means that transcendence is the constitutive structure of consciousness; that is, that consciousness is born supported by a being which is not itself. This is what we call the ontological proof. . . . Thus we have left pure appearance and have arrived at full being. Consciousness is a being whose existence posits its essence and inversely it is a consciousness of being, whose essence implies its existence; that is, in which appearance lays claim to *being*.[23]

It is precisely here that a phenomenological analysis of human being might disagree with Sartre's interpretation of human being as the being whose fundamental project is the desire for God, with the desire for being, constitutive of human freedom as nothingness, interpreted to be a desire for God. Sartre's account of the preontological comprehension may well not withstand criticism levied against his view of intentionality involving two distinctive modes of being apparently without unity, or against his view of freedom as the transcendental foundation of human existence within the mode of temporality, or against his prereflective cogito. Further, one might well accuse him of presenting a critique which does not follow from his preontological comprehension. Nevertheless, that does not mean that the preontological comprehension must lead to an ontology which explicitly brings the Transcendent to the fore, nor does it mean that his initially described phenomenological ontology demands such a Transcendent. Rather, what it could mean is that such a preontological comprehension and the description which accounts for it can go in differing directions, neutral to, if not exclusive of, the option for a Transcendent.

The question emerging here is whether phenomenology can come to the notion that God is ontologically constitutive of the human project. It may derive from existence the notion of limit, of finitude, of dependence, and of foun-

---

23. Jean-Paul Sartre, *Being and Nothingness*, p. LXI

dedness, but can it conclude more than that? It seems that the limits of phenomenological analysis are such that several interpretations of the above statement are viable. It may not be possible, based only on a phenomenological analysis, to justify interpretations springing from within a particular option over another interpretation springing from an opposite option. Or, at least, more must be said about the accessibility of phenomenology to the Transcendent. Further, perhaps the problem of freedom should not have been set up in Sartre's manner, beginning with a rupture between the pour soi and the en soi. But, again the question is necessary: does that presuppose or demand a God? The crucial question is whether phenomenology can, even in that context, derive a Transcendent for which it has not already opted? Would phenomenological description be essentially altered if the option was for the opposite belief, i.e., non God belief?

Perhaps such a phenomenological description leads necessarily to structures neutral to the ontic option of theism or atheism. Is there sufficient basis in Sartre's phenomenological descriptions, or in any phenomenology, to warrant the conclusion that the rereading should be in a different direction? Sartre certainly, as reflected in the quote from "Existentialism is a Humanism,"[24] wants to explore the consequences of a coherent atheistic position. Further, is it possible, after Kantian philosophy, to return to a Transcendent, even phenomenologically, without specifying precisely what it means and without a critical account of the access to the Transcendent? Perhaps this should be the direction of an attempt to overcome Sartre's quasi-polemical and uncomfortable atheism.

Therefore, although Sartre's phenomenological ontology in *Being and Nothingness* includes many incisive indict-

---

24. Jean-Paul Sartre,"Existence is a Humanism". See Chapter 4, p. [185] of this present study.

ments of any philosophy of the Transcendent, at the same time, it might serve the positive function of indicating limits of phenomenology in dealing with existence and a Transcendent. Such a phenomenology can reveal transcendence in relation to existence, even as constitutive of existence, but to specify a Transcendent in a religious sense as demanded by a phenomenology is perhaps to claim more than a descriptive interpretation can account for, thereby yielding more than is essentially related to the openness of existence. Such a phenomenology requires: first, great care in the way of speaking about *a Transcendent* especially attuned to today's hermeneutical situation; and, second, the admission that another option is possible, since the radical neutrality of essential structures allows for it, i.e., that on the ontic level, the other option is a viable possibility for beginning such reflection and becomes the hermeneutical situation to be reflected upon and from which reflection emerges. Thus, Sartre's treatment of the preontological level can be used for the purpose of indicating a certain limit to this level of analysis, which, once indicated, allows the further analysis to proceed with an explicit awareness of which option or presupposition is operative, but which has been seen in a more radical way. Sartre's analysis, however, at once demands further·clarification of existential phenomenology, for the oversimplistic dichotomy between the en soi and the pour soi is not adequate as an explication of being, and his statement that "transcendence is the constitutive structure of consciousness" needs further elaboration. Before returning to the theme of the neutral dimensions of existence below both options regarding the religious, then, it is necessary to briefly delve below Sartre's articulation by means of a broader and more fundamental consideration.

Existential phenomenology, in changing the meaning of intentionality and, at once, of sensation, understanding and imagination, has flatly rejected the transcendental element of Husserl's phenomenology because it fails to recast knowledge, experience and existence within the natal bond between humans and the world. For the early works of Merleau-Ponty, the originary level of experience, the realm of the primordial perceptual field, is the founding level of experience. In this context of vital intentionality, without reducing the role of experience to that of a spectator, the natal bond between humans and the world emerges in opposition to and reveals the inadequacy of both Husserl's idealism and any ontology which does not do justice to the independently existing element given in experience. This bond between nature and the human as "the quasi-organic relation of the perceiving subject and his world . . ."[25] gives access to the really real through perception. Thus, the meaning structure is that through which the real is encountered in a perceptual faith which lives in the belief that the world in which we live is the really real world.[26] Further, the originary level of unreflected experience is the foundation of all second-level reflection, all philosophy, all science—all expressions of a cultivated cultural level.

The earlier consideration of Merleau-Ponty's broadening and deepening of essential themes of phenomenology has set the stage for introducing the Heideggerian correlation between intentionality and transcendence in a manner different from that of Sartre. The discussion must now turn to the development of this theme in Heidegger in order to delve beneath Sartre's statement of the correlation at a level underlying the existential neutrality regarding the options of God belief.

A certain paradox emerges in Heidegger's various treatments of this relation between intentionality and transcen-

---

25. Maurice Merleau-Ponty, "The Primacy of Perception and Its Philosophical Consequences," in *The Primacy of Perception and Other Essays*, ed. by James Edie (Evanston, Illinois: Northwestern University Press, 1964), pp. 12–13.

26. Maurice Merleau-Ponty, *Phenomenology of Perception*, translated by Colin Smith (New York: The Humanities Press, 1962), Preface. p. XIII.

dence. On the one hand, intentionality has its ontological condition of possibility in transcendence, as shall be seen explicitly. Yet he states that "the intentional constitution of Dasein's comportment is precisely the ontological condition of the possibility of every and any transcendence."[27] How can intentionality be the ontological condition of possibility of transcendence while at once transcendence is the ontological condition of possibility of all intentional relations? This same ambiguity is reflected in Heidegger's claim that " . . . it is precisely intentionality and nothing else in which transcendence consists."[28] Furthermore, in indicating intentional comportment as "one of Dasein's basic constitutions,"[29] does not Heidegger seem to make intentionality fundamentally ontological? The basic question devolves into the relation between intentionality and the basic being structure of Dasein.[30] Further, as he says, "the intentional constitution of Dasein's comportments is precisely the ontological condition of the possibility of every and any transcendence. Transcendence, transcending, belongs to the essential nature of the being that exists (on the basis of transcendence) as intentional, that is, exists in the manner of dwelling among the extant."[31]

To unravel the ambiguity it must be seen that Heidegger considers the traditional view of intentionality, related to beings, to be an ontic comportment.[32] For Heidegger, intentionality as ontic relation is constitutive of transcendence as its structure of comportment and as its condition of possibility. Dasein's intentional comportment consti-

---

27. Martin Heidegger, *The Basic Problems of Phenomenology*, translated by Alaberft Hofstadter (Bloomington: Indiana University Press, 1982), p. 65.

28. Heidegger, *The Basic Problems of Phenomenology*, p. 63.

29. Heidegger, *The Basic Problems of Phenomenology*, p. 64.

30. Heidegger, *The Basic Problems of Phenomenology*, p. 64.

31. Heidegger, *The Basic Problems of Phenomenology*, p. 65.

32. Heidegger, *The Metaphysical Foundations of Logic*, translated by Michael Heim (Bloomington: Indiana University Press, 1984), 134.

tutes its transcendence to entities. However, there is more to it than that, for every such intentional transcendence as ontic also has belonging to it the understanding of the mode of being of what is intended in the intentum. Heidegger says, in the context of dealing with perception and its intentum: " . . . not only do intention and intentum belong to the intentionality of perception, but *so also does the understanding of the mode of being of what is intended in the intentum.*"[33] Accompanying the perception is an awareness of the being perceived, belonging to the intentionality of perception. Thus, on the concrete ontic level there is already an awareness of being which leads reflection to the expanded base of ontological transcendence as root of ontic transcendent intentionality. It can be further seen that being is grasped in the understanding of being, in being-in-the-world, as more basic ontologically. This "more proximate aspect of transcendence means the transcendence in which Dasein moves in an immediate way."[34]

Any ontic intentional transcendence has its origin in the fundamental ontological dimensions of Dasein and is possible only on the basis of being-in-the-world. As primal transcendence, being-in-the-world makes possible every intentional relation to beings. Further, this ontic intentional relation is based on a preliminary understanding of the being of beings and hence occurs in such a way that beings are in the "there" of Dasein, in and for Dasein's comportment with beings. Understanding-of-being, precisely as primordial transcendence or as being-in-the-world, grounds the ontic intentional relation. "If then primordial transcendence (being-in-the-world) makes possible the intentional relation and if the latter is, however, an ontic relation, and the relation to the ontic is grounded in the understanding-of-being, then there must be an intrinsic relationship between primordial

---

33. Heidegger, *The Basic Problems of Phenomenology*, p. 71.
34. Heidegger, *The Metaphysical Foundations of Logic*, p. 135.

transcendence and the understanding-of-being. They must in the end be one and the same."[35]

It is precisely this fundamental distinction made by Heidegger between intentionally constituted ontic transcendence and ontological, primordial, grounding transcendence that must be brought together with Merleau-Ponty's use of the distinction between intentionality of acts and operative intentionality. Merleau-Ponty can be seen to relate operative intentionality—in the context of his extensions of understanding, intentionality, meaning and the transcendental—to Heidegger's transcendence. In referring to this deeper, operative intentionality, Merleau-Ponty indicates it as that which "others have called existence"[36] and which "Heidegger has called transcendence."[37] While intentionality constitutes transcendence on the level of concrete existence, this ontic level is not the most originary structure of human being. Intentionality, as ontic transcendence, is possible only on the basis of original transcendence as being-in-the-world. Hence, it must be clearly understood precisely how transcendence consists in intentionality and that this is intentionality within being. Merleau-Ponty says: "The whole Husserlian analysis is blocked by the framework of acts which impose upon it the philosophy of *consciousness*. It is necessary to take up again and develop the *fungierende* or *latent* intentionality which is the intentionality within being."[38] It is this level which Sartre's ontology fails to reach, therefore allowing the truncated dichotomy between en soi and pour soi.

The foundational character of originary transcendence can be instructive for this whole study. For what was needed in Ricoeur's treatment of existence was a structural character neutral to the presuppositional prejudice of fal-

35. Heidegger, *The Metaphysical Foundations of Logic*, 135–136.
36. Merleau-Ponty, *Phenomenology of Perception*, p. 121, n. 5.
37. Merleau-Ponty, *Phenomenology of Perception*, p. 418.
38. Merleau-Ponty, *The Visible and the Invisible*, p. 244.

lenness, leaving existence, even as self-transcendence, intact. The positive contribution from Sartre's teaching has been superceded by Heidegger's originary transcendence. Thus, this brief account of Heidegger's originary transcendence allows us at this point to return to the development of the religious in existence.

The ontic being-in-the-world of Dasein can be seen to have a common ontological structure, no matter which concrete worlds are dealt with. If the religious option, whether positive or negative regarding God, is the context of the investigation, then the possibility is open to interpret the ontic in either way. Nevertheless, the ontological structures and process are the same for either consideration. And what is spoken of, within the God belief option, as the Sacred and as God can only be spoken of in indirect language, as Ricoeur so well says. The discussion will next look at this aspect of Ricoeur's thinking, which has become so fundamental to the works of the theologians mentioned in Chapter Three.

CHAPTER FIVE

Finite Religious Existence, Indirect Expressions, and Totality

The present study has shown that belief in God cannot be adequately established by means of descriptive phenomenology, which must preserve a certain neutrality within religious existence. It is possible, however, to have an access to totality through indirect language, as has been mentioned. This chapter attempts to focus further on this access to totality and on the consequences of the philosophical limit placed upon human reason in its demand for totality within finite existence. The discussion will focus primarily upon Ricoeur's developments within this context, since his philosophy is at the heart of the problematics and has thus been heeded by the best treatments of the problem within recent philosophical theology. This chapter will attempt to bring the reflection upon the foundations and eidetic dimensions of the religious dimensions of existence within being-in-the-world to its indirect expression. A phenomenological interpretation of existence, as was seen in Chapter Three, still remains neutral to any objective religious realm, in the process of delving into the hermeneutic situation (as the totality of presuppositions) of existence. After some discussion of that level, and a critique of phenomenological theology to found theological reflection—especially within a Christian tradition—a more explicit account is rendered via a critique of a certain view of human existence as fallen, and via a somewhat creative interpretation of existence using Heidegger, Merleau-Ponty, Sartre and Ricoeur as points of departure, insofar as they illustrate this dimension of existence and insofar as their existential phenomenology is able to be appropriated in an analysis of religious existence which remains true to the rigor of this analysis as phenomenological interpretation.

Paul Ricoeur has continually and consistently unfolded his philosophy within the keen awareness of, and attunement to, the Kantian philosophy of limits, yet without reducing his philosophy to that of Kant. This is the context of his creative reinterpretation of the Kantian limit idea which, as such, does not provide an object of experience and is not constitutive of knowledge, but which can serve a regulative role in directing reason to totality and to completion regarding an unconditioned.[1]

The limit function is not overlooked even in this contemporary philosophy which denies the dichotomy between the phenomenon and the noumenon, between the finite and the infinite, and between freedom and nature. Rather, although Husserl employed phenomenology, overcoming certain weaknesses of neo-Kantianism, it is still Kant who limited and founded phenomenology in relation especially to the unconditioned of reason. "Husserl *did* phenomenology, but Kant *limited* and *founded* it."[2] The limit is manifest in experience, language and concept, and in the preconceptual comprehension of existence. Hence the totality is not given exhaustively, and the fullness of meaning is not encompassed completely, so that their revelation is ongoing and continuous. It is necessary to explore further the significance of the Kantian limit imposed by reason on knowledge.

Appropriating Kant's doctrine, Ricoeur contends that objective knowledge is the labor of understanding (*verstand*), but understanding does not exhaust the power of reason (*vernunft*) which remains the function of the unconditioned. This distance and this tension between reason, as the function of the unconditioned, and understanding, as

---

1. Paul Ricoeur, "What Does Humanism Mean?", pp. 85–87.
2. Ricoeur, *Husserl, Analysis of His Phenomenology*, p. 201.

the function of conditioned knowledge, find an expression in the notion of *limit*, which for Kant is not to be identified with boundary. This concept of "limit" does not primarily imply that our knowledge is limited, but, rather, that the quest for the unconditioned puts limits on the claim of objective knowledge. " 'Limit' is not a fact, but an act,"[3] meaning that in its quest for the unconditioned, reason actively puts limits on the claim of objective knowledge to become absolute. Ricoeur, however, wants to give to the limit-concept of Kant a less negative function than this prohibition addressed by reason to the claim of objective knowledge to absolutize itself. Rather, for Ricoeur, the "empty" requirement of an Unconditioned finds a certain fulfillment in the indirect presentation of metaphorical language, which says what things are *like* rather than what things *are*, and that the "is like" implies an "is not."[4] It is precisely on this level that Ricoeur can introduce his own religious concerns and preserve a religious sense of the Sacred.

In the present context, however, the philosophy of limits dwells primarily on the limits which are essential to the philosophy of human existence within reason's quest for totality and for completeness. As Ricoeur says: "I think everything and I demand everything, but I am never able to know it. Kant only applied to cosmology his golden rule of the limiting function of the concept of the thing-in-itself."[5] He wants to extend this application to apply, in the present context, to the totality of man[6] and to the totality of history."[7]

---

3. Paul Ricoeur, "Biblical Hermeneutics," *Semeia* IV, 1975, p. 142.

4. Ricoeur, "Biblical Hermeneutics," p. 142.

5. Ricoeur, "What Does Humanism Mean?", p. 86.

6. Ricoeur, *Fallible Man* p. 75. "That explains why our method will consist rather in taking the idea of totality as a task, as a directive idea in the Kantian sense, as a demand for totalization. We shall try to make this demand work in a direction opposed to that of radicality or purity which regulated our first investigation."

7. Ricoeur, "What Does Humanism Mean?", p. 86. "But it is necessary

Ricoeur further reminds us that according to the *Critique of Practical Reason*, the only extension of our knowledge is practical, concerning the connection between freedom and the law. However, he extends ethics beyond the narrowness of morality or of the ideal of duty and obligation:

> If ethics covers the whole field of our travel from bondage to freedom, . . . if ethics is the theory of the mediation through which we fulfill our desire to be, our effort to exist, then an ethical interpretation of poetic and religious discourse has no reductive effect. It opens, on the contrary, a fruitful dialogue between ethics and hermeneutics. The *concept*, once more, is on the side of a philosophical ethics, whether we conceive ethics in terms of norms, values, institutions, or in terms of creativity, free expression, permanent revolution, etc. Now these concepts are *empty* without their indirect presentation in symbols, parables, and myths. It is the task of hermeneutics to disentangle from the "world" of the texts, their implicit "project" for existence, their indirect "proposition" of new modes of being. These intuitions are *blind* to the extent that ethical concepts are *empty*. Hermeneutics has finished its job when it has opened the eyes and the ears, i.e., when it has displayed before our imagination the figures of our authentic existence. It is the task of ethics to articulate its coherent discourse by listening to what the poet says.[8]

The advance of this extended ethic through a "philosophy of the will" ultimately leads Ricoeur to address Kant's resolution of the third antinomy between freedom and natural necessity.[9] In turning to the complex problem

---

to apply to the totality of history this *limiting* role of the ideal of its total meaning and to raise it up against all pretensions that would say what this total meaning is." p. 140

8. Ricoeur, "Biblical Hermeneutics," p. 144.

9. For a development of the resolution of the antinomy between freedom and necessity by Ricoeur and by Heidegger, see Patrick Lyall Bourgeois and Frank Schalow, "Freedom, Finitude, and Totality: Ricoeur and Heidegger," *The Journal of the British Society for Phenomenology*, vol. 18, No. 3, Oct. 1987.

of resolving the third antinomy of Kant, it is necessary to recall further certain fundamental adaptations made by Ricoeur in his creative reinterpretation of Kantian philosophy. First of all, in giving a more positive interpretation of role to the limit-concept than Kant, Ricoeur has fundamentally altered the Kantian radical dichotomy between phenomenon and noumenon. For, after all, the Kantian noumenon as a limiting concept is mainly negative in the sense that it is not a possible object of sense-perception. If a noumenon or a thing-in-itself becomes in any way not only a non-phenomenon, but something which somehow is accessible to human experience, then the concept is no longer a limiting concept in the strictly negative sense. Therefore, in giving even indirect access to what Kant refers to as ideas or as limiting concepts, Ricoeur seeks a new basis for mediating the dichotomy between the noumenal and the phenomenal, thereby giving access to a totality not allowed for, or envisioned by, Kant. Ricoeur, however, does not fall into the trap of considering the totality to be an object of experience or constitutive of experience. Rather, he uses the limiting concept as regulative in such a way as to allow for and, indeed, to *demand* that reason think from the indirect expressions the whole of man and the totality of reality. For it is only as a regulative idea that the totality and the unity of man along with the Sacred are given to thought.

Still following Kant, Ricoeur speaks of the "the spirit" (*Geist*) in an aesthetic sense, as "the life-giving principle of the mind (*Gemut*)."[10] The ideas given by reason to the imagination assign a task to the interplay (game) between imagination and understanding, forcing the understanding to think more. Ricoeur has, then, opened up Kant's doctrine on several crucial points: first, the indirect ex-

---

10. Paul Ricoeur, *The Rule of Metaphor*, translated by Robert Czerny with Kathleen McLaughlin and John Costello, SJ (Toronto: University of Toronto Press, 1977), p. 303.

pressions, symbols, metaphors, myths and narrative discourse provide reason with an indirect access to the total and to the unconditioned; second, the illusion of reason in attempting to make its ideas an object of experience is overcome, not by denying the illusion, but by buying into another access; third, the speculative orientation of reason, rooted in the drive on the part of reason to unity and totality, is the outgrowth of the tendency to found— although in a limited way—the knowledge of understanding, but now nourished by means of the indirect expressions, presented to the understanding for thought, and demanding totality of reason from that "thinking more" of understanding. Thus, within that game between understanding and imagination, and their tasks assigned by the Ideas of reason, the condition making speculative thought possible emerges. Yet the necessity of that thought arises from the reason itself, in affording the life-giving principle to the mind, and, in so doing, producing the conditions which make possible what is necessary from reason, i.e., speculative thought. This leads to a speculative discourse responding to and ontologically clarifying the postulate of reference within poetic discourse.[11]

Within the sphere of poetics, in metaphorical and narrative discourse, semantic innovation is placed in the Kantian productive imagination in its role of schematism. It is the work of the productive imagination to perceive resemblance in terms at first seen apart and then brought together by inaugurating the similarity between them. "This consists of schematizing the synthetic operation, of figuring the predicative assimilation from whence results the semantic innovation."[12] In this context, however, Ricoeur wants to cut beneath the imaginative synthesis of providing schemata for the rules of understanding in uni-

---

11. Ricoeur, *The Rule of Metaphor*, p. 303.
12. Paul Ricoeur, *Time and Narrative*, Vol. I, trans. by Kathleen McLaughlin and David Pellauer, (Chicago: The University of Chicago Press, 1984), p. x.

fying the manifold of sense for objective knowledge. This role of creative imagination cannot be separated from the connection between symbols and metaphors for Ricoeur, and the relation between the symbol and metaphor is essential with regard to creativity in semantic innovation of the imagination, for symbols are bound to spirit and to desire. Continuous with symbols, metaphors stress the unbound creativity in expressions with double meaning in the overall context of polysemy. Thus, looked at from that direction, the imagination in its role of schematism is the source of semantic innovation.[13] However, looked at from the perspective of reason, it is reason (spirit) which gives to the imagination the ideas which stimulate creative thought, which, in "thinking more," cannot ever be adequate to the idea. Therefore, the demand for totality within the context of a bond to existence, through desire and spirit, allows a glimpse again at the infinite quest within a finite situation. It is beneficial to pursue this line of thought further in the direction of the productive imagination and its schematism, for it is here that we see Ricoeur's own philosophic framework, both as Kantian and as contemporary, undercutting and underlying all of his philosophy of the will and myriad excursions into dialogue with other philosophies.

It is necessary to pursue further this extended role of the productive imagination in schematism, following Ricoeur's interpretation of Kant:

> It will be recalled that I compared the "grasping together" characteristic of the configurational act to judgment as

---

13. "But if we follow Kant rather than Hume, I mean the theory of schematism and that of productive imagination, we have to look at the imagination as the place of nascent meanings and categories, rather than as the place of fading impressions. . . . And could we not say by anticipation that imagination is the emergence of conceptual meaning through the interplay between sameness and difference? Metaphor would be the place in discourse where this emergence may be detected because sameness and difference are in conflict." Paul Ricoeur, "Creativity in Language," *Philosophy Today*, vol. 17, No. 2, Summer 1973, p. 109.

understood by Kant. Remaining in a Kantian vein, we ought not to hesitate in comparing the production of the configurational act to the work of the productive imagination. This latter must be understood not as a psychologizing faculty but as a transcendental one. The productive imagination is not only rule-governed, it constitutes the generative matrix of rules. In Kant's first *Critique*, the categories of the understanding are first schematized by the productive imagination. The schematism has this power because the productive imagination fundamentally has a synthetic function. It connects understanding and intuition by engendering syntheses that are intellectual and intuitive at the same time. Emplotment, too, engenders a mixed intelligibility between what has been called the point, theme, or thought of a story, and the intuitive presentation of circumstances, characters, episodes, and changes of fortune that make up the denouement. In this way, we may speak of a schematism of the narrative function. . . .

This schematism, in turn, is constituted within a history that has all the characteristics of a tradition. Let us understand by this term not the inert transmission of some already dead deposit of material but the living transmission of an innovation always capable of being reactivated by a return to the most creative moments of poetic activity. So understood, traditionality enriches the relationship between plot and time with a new feature.[14]

He says further: "However Kant only recognized those determinations of time that contribute to the objective constitution of the physical world. The schematism of the narrative function implies determinations of new genre which are precisely the ones we have just designated by the dialectic of the episodic characteristics and the configuring of emplotment."[15] We see Ricoeur expanding on the Kantian determination of time to include, within the context of indirect expressions, the whole of the narrative

---

14. Ricoeur, *Time and Narrative*, vol. I, p. 68.
15. Ricoeur, *Time and Narrative*, p. 244, n. 18.

function, which allows for expressing new worlds in texts. Such expression is correlated to the other end of the hermeneutical arch as the original appropriation of the latent world of the text, expanding the world of the listener. Such ontic aspects of existence must be further investigated in terms of the ontic access to the Sacred explored in earlier works by Ricoeur, and culminating only now in his most recent works, which deal with the world of the text and narrative discourse. In overcoming the supposed phenomenological subjectivism of Husserl, Ricoeur has refocused on the openness and rootedness of existence, and exposed the significance of the decenteredness of the Cogito in terms of its twofold dependence upon desire and upon spirit. This ontic existential dependence has its roots in a further dependence on the ultimate *telos* and *arche*, the Sacred.

Ricoeur has to begin this analysis by pointing out that the Totally Other ceases to be Totally Other as other as soon as it addresses me. But in becoming an event in the human word, the Totally-Other can only be recognized in the movement of interpretation, and thus can be arrived at in the context of the dialectic between archeology and teleology. "It is as horizon of my archeology and as horizon of my teleology that creation and eschatology are announced."[16] Ricoeur considers this *arche* and this *telos* as the horizon of my roots and as the horizon of my intentions, respectively. This is how he arrives at the ultimate *arche* and *telos*, at the root of roots and the supreme of the supreme. The movement or extension, then, can be followed in both directions, that of the transition from the phenomenology of the spirit and from the psychoanalysis of Freud to the phenomenology of the Sacred. At this point, however, a fundamental objection to the pivotal extension of the Kantian limit concept must be confronted

---

16. Ricoeur, *Time and Narrative*, p. 526.

as preliminary for discussing the limits of such a philosophy and its view of human existence.

In integrating the positive function of the limit concept with the indirect access to the total and unconditioned, the serious objection emerges as to whether this indirect access simply recasts the Kantian phenomenal/noumenal dichotomy, but now one place removed from Kant's formulation, i.e., does he reintroduce it with the indirect access to the "ultimate arche," "ultimate telos," and "totally other" as Sacred? A brief discussion on the access to being in the context of the phenomenal/noumenal distinction is therefore in order.

First, Ricoeur's is not a reductive and quasi-atomistic interpretation of our ontic access to things in perception. He concurs with and fosters an existential phenomenology which understands that the phenomenon is the appearance of the thing, and that in the apprehension of the thing there is a comprehension of the being of the perceived. In the phenomenological move to the thing itself, and to the being of the thing, the radical split between the phenomenon and the noumenon is overcome. For Kantian philosophy, there is no knowledge of the noumenal, since the noumena, the things themselves, are entities to which no objects of experience can ever correspond, while "phenomena" are or can be objects of experience. It is the objects of experience which are, for Kant, the only objects which can be known, since knowledge arises from the application of the categories, and the categories cannot be applied to anything outside possible objective experience. Thus, it is Kant's non-spectator view of knowledge which leads, ultimately, to the noumenal-phenomenal distinction.

Existential phenomenology in general, and Ricoeur's philosophy in particular, are more radically non-spectator than Kantian philosophy. First, it must be seen that existential philosophy, in deepening the notion of intentionality to the level of an operative intentionality already at work before any judgment, recasts the celebrated themes, and brings the demands of the phenomenal-noumenal distinction to a more radical level in phenomenology. In overcoming the phenomenal-noumenal dichotomy, the structure of the phenomena are, at the originary level, structures of existence. The really real, rather than an inaccessible underlying noumenal X, is the matrix of existence of being-in-the-world. What appears on this primordial level of openness as real is not exhausted in its appearance. For Ricoeur, the sense of being and of my own being, in being-in-the-world, becomes the sense through which the Sacred becomes ontically accessible. So the phenomenal-noumenal break is overcome and ontological presence engendered. However, is the break reintroduced with the indirect access to the Sacred? To deal adequately with this objection, Ricoeur's unequivocal rejection of the tendency to reify and objectify the Sacred must be considered.

The positive function of the limit concept, as the indirect access to the total or to the Sacred, however, must be explicitly shown not to militate against overcoming the phenomenal-noumenal distinction, but rather to demand a recognition of a philosophical limit placed on this level. First of all, it goes beyond the scope of a philosophical reflection to deal with a specific religious response within a specific faith option. More fundamentally, however, it must be admitted that the existential and ontological structures yielded by philosophical reflection do not yield any eidetic relation to God, to the Sacred, or to any such object. Rather, what is found—which is quite compatible with the above discussion on overcoming the dichotomy between the noumenal and phenomenal—is a preconceptual ontological openness to being through the occurrence of world and through the sense of being, which can be the vehicle or mediator for symbols or metaphors as indirect expressions leading further.

The symbols of the Sacred designate the impact of a

reality in culture which the movement of culture cannot contain. It serves as an attraction or as an appeal to the whole succession of figures of culture, as a *telos*. "The sacred is its eschatology; it is the horizon which reflection does not understand, does not encompass. . . ."[17] It is by its reflection on the immanent teleology of the succession of figures that the Sacred discerns that philosophy of spirit or culture as its eschatology.[18]

Likewise, the phenomenology of the Sacred, with its symbols, is related to psychoanalysis in the same function of horizon. Thus it becomes the *arche* of every *arche*. It is necessary for the problem of faith to demand demystification in order not to fall back into the antithesis prior to the dialectic. This need arises because of the tendency of the horizon to be converted into an object; therefore, Ricoeur sees the manner of treatment of illusion by Freud, Marx and Nietzsche as on a second level. This tendency to convert the horizon into an object, or this process of objectivation, is a more fundamental level of illusion and is a return to the illusion of reason in the way Kant saw it. For Ricoeur, this is at the same time the birth of metaphysics and of religions: "of metaphysics which makes God a supreme being; of religion which treats the Sacred as a new sphere of objects, of institutions, and of powers now inscribed in the world of immanence, of the objective spirit, alongside objects, institutions, and powers of the economic, political, and cultural spheres."[19]

It is this objectivation of faith which brings faith into the sphere of illusion, and is thus the subject of an hermentutic of the reductive style.[20] Freudianism is one of these. This reductive hermeneutics today has to become a cultural phenomenon. It must demystify the idols to which this

17. Ricoeur, *Time and Narrative*, p. 529.
18. Ricoeur, *Time and Narrative*, p. 528.
19. Ricoeur, *Time and Narrative*, p. 530.
20. Ricoeur, *Time and Narrative*, p. 529.

tendency to objectivation leads. "That is why it is always necessary for the idol to die in order for the symbol to live."[21] The symbol's richness is in its ambiguity and it is this ambiguity which makes possible the different valencies giving rise to different interpretations. "The 'symbol gives rise to thought,' but is also the birth of the idol: that is why the critique of the idol remains the condition of the conquest of the symbol."[22] Thus, the Kantian noumenal is avoided, and the limits of human access within existence are admitted.

This response to the objection concerning the phenomenal/noumenal break provides the occasion for a fundamental critical adjustment in Ricoeur's basic philosophy of existence. Ricoeur's philosophical focus on religious symbols and their underlying meaning causes no problem insofar as a philosophic task is undertaken. He does more than that, however, by letting assumed religious content slip into the philosophical hermeneutical situation of his philosophical fore-comprehension. Therefore religious content is not simply looked at, but assumed, and precisely within his philosophy. This has led him to accept, with Kant, an overly religious overtone to his interpretation of radical evil as a necessary and constitutive aspect of existential freedom, requiring that human existence be fallen. It is precisely this assumed stance within which Ricoeur begins his analysis of the ontic aspect of existence, and this requires further reflection.

Ricoeur's view of existence required an adjustment in three phases for philosophical purity and radicality: first, there is a need to explicate the faith option within which much of his philosophy of existence is developed in order to liberate existence *philosophically* from its prejudice; second, within that context, radical evil must be extricated

---

21. Ricoeur, *Time and Narrative*, p. 531.
22. Ricoeur, *Time and Narrative*, p. 543.

from its necessarily constitutive role in existential freedom; and third, the resultant moral neutrality of existence must liberate human existence from fallenness as its necessary constitution, so that existence as innocent, fallen, and recreated can be seen to share the same existential structure. This discussion must turn briefly to the aforementioned options in order to clarify the adjustments needed in Ricoeur's philosophy of existence.

Within reflection upon the general realm of religious existence and upon the Sacred, several levels of option to believe religiously can be distinguished: that of the explicit faith commitment of a specific religion concretely expressed in a particular denomination in its concrete situation and with its own tradition; second, that of the faith of the theist or atheist, more basic than the first option and presupposed by it; and finally, the structural dimension as the foundation of all these levels of options. Inevitably, the question must be posed as to whether Ricoeur's phenomenology has not tended to presuppose in some way the content of a specific religious faith with its subtly implicit metaphysics of freedom, without sufficient rational reflective scrutiny.

A phenomenological analysis, delving into the fundamental level of existence as the root and foundation of religious experience below the subject and object disjunction, shows the fundamental openness at the heart of human existence as the foundation of all experience, even of religious experience. However, it becomes clear that for such a phenomenological reflection on this foundational level, the structures of existence are neutral to God belief or God nonbelief. Religious beliefs, practices and intepretations exist within an option: i.e., the option for God belief, in contrast to the option against God belief, which also contains the religious aspect of experience as essential.[23] At this foundational level of the existential

---

23. See Patrick L. Bourgeois, "Religious Experience and the Philosophical Radicalization of Phenomenological Theology," *Proceedings of the*

openness of man's being-in-the-world, the nature of the root of knowledge and the fundamental dimensions of being can be descriptively interpreted without presupposition of theism or atheism reigning supreme at the outset. Further, the limits of this level, especially in relation to the realm of presuppositions with which we begin philosophy, can be made thematic, but in relation to the nature and the claims of religious experience.

A phenomenology of religious experience separates the essential structures of religious existence from the dimensions of religious experience which are not essential to existence. Although some such dimensions of religious experience may indeed be essential to religious experience of a particular type within a particular option, this does not necessitate their being essential to religious existence as such. What this means is that such a phenomenology of religious experience demands the liberation of the interpretation of the bond of human being to being, in being-in-the-world, from even a presuppositional tie to the Sacred as *necessarily* involving an absolute transcendent order. Such an analysis must allow for the interpretation of this bond to the Sacred even as absolute, as a possibility, but not as an eidetic aspect of existence. It therefore requires that the same existential structure be essential to the atheistic life as well as to the theistic life. Thus, the essential and neutral structures of existence have emerged as central to existence whether it be ontically expressed as theistic or as atheistic. The Gordian knot of this paradox is intertwined with the realization that the whole person, the volitional and passional dimensions of existence included, are at the root of either belief on the presuppositional level, even though there is not apodictic evidence justifying such a belief before it is accepted. However, that does not preclude reflection making sense out of such a commitment in the context of the whole of life and the whole of reality, and explicitly confirming the position after the presuppositional strata are reflectively brought to light.

Ricoeur has chosen to look at religious symbols within a theistic option and within a specific tradition. Admitting this, he then allows certain assumed philosophical tenets full play—as, for instance, radical evil and the captive will, and hope of regenaration. A more neutral account is necessary, posing the corrective element to Ricoeur's thought. The "already there" of evil[24] and "the prior captivity, which makes it so that I must do evil"[25] can be re-placed or put on a better philosophical base than the Kantian notion of radical evil. Rather, philosophically, these expressions tell us that humans are not determined and that freedom is capable of mistakes, error and evil. Thus, reinterpreted, Ricoeur's statement that "I claim that my freedom has already made itself non-free"[26] means that freedom is already human, and therefore must be actualized in the finite. This reinterpretation places, within the existential structures, a neutrality common to innocent, fallen, and recreated existence.

It is necessary to criticize Ricoeur for remaining too Kantian in spite of his fundamental opposition to Kant's view of the place of evil in man. In such a critique, what emerges is the view that the structures of human existence are, like the eidetic structures, equally foundational for innocent, fallen, and regenerated existence, because it is precisely existence which is neutral to all of these, and the bracketing of fault, innocence, passion and Transcendence should be maintained in a pure reflection on existence. For existence is not only manifest as fallen, but also conditions

---

American Catholic Philosophical Association, 1981; and Patrick L. Bourgeois, "Religious Existence and the Philosophical Radicalization of Phenomenological Theology," *Proceedings of the American Catholic Philosophical Association*, 1984.
p. 155
    24. Paul Ricoeur, *The Conflict of Interpretations*, p. 435.
    25. Ricoeur, *The Conflict of Interpretations*, p. 436.
    26. Ricoeur, *The Conflict of Interpretations*, p. 436.

which make evil will possible are equally the conditions which make good will possible.

The existential conditions of the possibility of fallenness, in the sense of the evil heart or hardened heart—or, in more Kantian terms, the evil of the maxim of the will—are the same existential conditions or structures of the good will and the seeking of the highest good, and of regeneration to a new life. To consider the fallenness accidental to the essential structures of willing, then, may still be too Kantian for a contemporary philosophy, which should go the further step and consider fallenness as a possibility instead of as a necessity belonging to the existential structure of synthesis. This altered view does not rule out the privileged place of the mythic of evil but, rather, puts it within the context of the fullness and excess of meaning on the concrete level, on an equal footing with the mythic of innocence and of regeneration, all on the concrete level, without overplaying or overinterpreting its place in the philosophical analysis of human existence.

Hence it can be seen how the hermeneutics of existence fits into Ricoeur's philosophy of limits within the limits of reason. First, it is limited, within the realm of existence, to elements accidental to the essential structures of man. Even the creative and poetic interpretation, in its fictive recreation of possible worlds to be appropriated or of worlds to be expressed in texts, is within the limits of being-in-the-world, as it deals with conditions of existence which, as such, are nonessential to the abstract nature of man. In this sense, the hermeneutic of existence is not eidetic.

This is why, for Ricoeur, the eidetics of the human yields an abstract human prescinding from the actual conditions of existence. According to the preface to *Fallible Man*,[27] it is the "undifferentiated keyboard" upon which is reverberated the various instances of human existences, as inno-

---

27. Ricoeur, *Fallible Man*, p. xvi.

cent, fallen, and regenerated in redemption. The attempt to separate the eidetic from the existential dimensions of humans establishes the merely accidental character of existence as fallen, avoiding the danger of ontologizing the fault in the human existential constitution. It is precisely the tension and differences between the abstract human and existing human, or, in another context, between the eidetics of the will and the pure reflection on the existential structures of the human, which proves decisive for Ricoeur.

Such an abstraction is admittedly a limitation. It is only later, in the releasing of the abstraction, that the fuller understanding of humans and their structures can be grasped. However, Ricoeur considers the abstraction to supply a guiding limit for fundamental ontology. Without such a limit, there is a danger of existential monism, which Ricoeur rejects, and a tendency to ontologize accidental aspects of the empirical existence of humans, assuming agreement with Ricoeur regarding the radicality of evil in human freedom, and this as accidental to the human eidetic structures. Thus Ricoeur, beginning with an eidetics, clears the way for a grasp of the being of the human condition in fundamental ontology. This becomes clear from the fundamental principle yielded by this pure description, the polemical unity of humans as a regulative idea. It is our contention that the ontology allowed for should be slightly different than the one he envisions, demanding an essential adjustment in his view of the locus of evil in the existential structures of existence.

It must be admitted that Ricoeur should perhaps be more open to a basic level of unity and a neutral place for the possibility of evil and of good in the existential possibilities of Dasein. These can be maintained without compromising his philosophic conviction, different from that of Heidegger, of human existence as the synthesis of finite and infinite, and of the necessity to treat the ontic level of existence more extensively and openly than Heidegger does. Nor does it necessarily preclude his view, against Heidegger, of the synthesis in humans between the infinite and the finite. It would, however, both prevent an ontologizing of the Sacred, a concern dear to Ricoeur and, at once, render a philosophically more plausible account of human existence, opening the way for a fundamental ontology and for ontology.

It is precisely the fundamental and constitutive comprehension of being, as primordial transcendence or as being-in-the-world, which grounds ontic intentional relations. Further, quite compatible with the above discussion on overcoming the dichotomy between the noumenal and phenomenal realms, what is found is a preconceptual ontological openness to being through the occurrence of world and through the sense of being, which can be the vehicle or mediator for symbols or metaphors as indirect expressions leading further than their ontic manifestions. In this context, the symbol's structure and ontological sense allow the ontic to introduce the ontological dimension. For once the option for the Sacred is made on the ontic level, in reason's demand for totality and in the task of the understanding to think more, using the imagination's presentation to it from spirit (Geist), access to the being revealed in being-in-the-world reaches toward primordial, ontological, grounding transcendence constitutive of Dasein, which underlies intentionally constituted ontic transcendence. The question emerges again whether this indirect, ontological access consequent to a fundamental option misleads us if we immediately call it *being*. Being, the horizon of which is primordial time, can be seen to be grasped in its truth and sense, and only then can it be reinterpreted in the light of the holy or of the divine or of the Sacred. Therefore, the fundamental openness of Dasein in transcendence to world is access to being, which, in turn, and within a further option, is access to the Sacred. This latter, as expressed in symbols, contains the fundamental ontological structure as does any instance of being-in-the-world, and must not too quickly be reduced to a being. Thus the specifically ontic-ontological complexity and ambiguity emerges. For, while the Sacred in relation to human existence, not eidetic to existence, is not ontological, it presupposes the ontological structures of being-in-the-world and introduces reflection on the religious to the ontological, yet it presupposes a further ontic option based on the ontological openness of Dasein. Reason can therefore be satisfied in its demand for totality; the demand for the religious is satisfied, even though tenuously, but the further significance of the Sacred as it reveals being further than the being of finite existence is accessible only indirectly, and requires further thinking regarding the truth of being manifest in symbols. The Sacred, even ontically, makes sense only within the religious option. In making ontological sense within the religious option, it makes sense as something beyond the being accessible through world, yet it is accessible only through world and being-in-the-world, and only indirectly accessible.

This book has attempted to address a fundamental aspect of the philosophical problem emerging from the religious dimension of human experience and existence. In so doing, the analysis has served as a basic philosophical analysis into the presuppositional base from which philosophical reflection as such proceeds and to which it inevitably returns. It has delved into the philosophical substrate for phenomenological theology by employing a phenomenology of religious experience and existence to explicate the openness and transcendence of existence, thereby achieving a radicalization of phenomenology in theology, and, at once, allowing us to grasp the place of juncture between a viable existential phenomenology within a contemporary worldview and phenomenological theology. Further, this analysis has uncovered serious limits on this descriptive level of method, since it has been explicitly found through descriptive interpretation that a basic level of human existence will be seen to ground both theistic and atheistic responses, and to ground the limit philosophy within which both emerge. It has been found that a phenomenological method is able to provide a fundamental vision of the prephilosophical level which grounds all levels of activity and experience. This vantage point must be won with great effort, and is not merely a given. The change of focus of phenomenology, the illusive reduction—though not the monstrosities people have made them out to be—cannot be achieved without care for presuppositions. It has been the precise task of this study to enter into the presuppositions by means of the phenomenological descriptions of experience and of existence made possible by the carefully engaged reduction, imaginative variation, and eidetic analyses yielding the essential structural dimensions of religious experience and of religious existence.

It has been found that at this foundational level of the existential openness of human being-in-the-world, the nature of the root of knowledge and the fundamental dimension of being can be descriptively interpreted without the presuppositions of theism or of atheism reigning supreme at the outset. Further, the limits of this level, especially in relation to the realm of presupposition with which we begin philosophy, have been made thematic, but in relation to the nature and the claim of religious experience. The neutrality, seen within the essential dimensions of experience and of existence, requires of a radical foundation for theological reflection the advertence to that level, and for philosophical adequacy, it requires further philosophical explication. As such, this analysis has shown both the philosophical viability and inadequacy of recent phenomenological theology. This present study has not attempted to destroy or even to qualify that theological manner of interpretation. Rather, it has attempted to delve deeper, in a strictly philosophical way, to the foundational possibility latent in that presuppositional level of faith, uncovering an essential structure central to religious options as such.

As mentioned at the end of the Introduction, this study attempts to have only the first word and not the final word. As such, it lays open the possibility and even the demand for a reflection of an entirely different nature which deals with religious questions in an entirely different manner. In admitting the limits of a descriptive interpretation of phenomenology, the intention has not been to preclude another level of philosophical discourse, such as the speculative, undertaking tasks not possible for a descriptive method. Such a speculative philosophy would advance beyond the limits of this study and would yield a different level of interpretation.

Index

Index

adjustment, 29, 30–33, 49, 50, 58, 62.
affective, 45, 51, 55.
Alypius, 39.
atheism, 5, 7, 8, 12, 27, 28, 33, 36, 59, 60, 73, 74, 100, 120, 121, 127.
Augustine, 36, 39 & ff, 42, 62.

Brentano, 15n.10.

character, 96.
Christ, 38–42, 62.
cognitive, 45, 84n.2.
conversion, 36, 38, 42, 46, 48, 49.

descriptive, 2.
Dewey, J., 1–2, 7, 18–19, 21, 22, 25, 26, 27–33, 34, 45, 47, 51, 53, 63, 74, 98.
dogmatic, 11, 12.
dualism, 83.

emotion, 50.
epistemic, 11.
eschatology, 118.
evil, 95, 96, 97, 119, 123, 124.

fallenness, 93, 97.
fault, 95.
fanaticism, 8–9.
Farley, E., 8n.2, 72, 74, 76–78.
feeling, 52, 53, 56.
Freud, 118.

Gilkey, Langdon, 8n.2, 54, 64, 68, 69, 72, 74–80.

happiness, 96.
Heidegger, 82, 85n.3, 86–87, 92, 94, 95, 97, 98, 103, 124.
humanism, 5, 81–91, 100.
Hume, 113n.13.
Husserl, 14n.8, 15n.9 and n.10.
hypothesis, 25, 26.

imagination, 6, 16n.11, 32–33, 37, 51–52, 91, 96, 97, 110, 111, 113, 114, 125.
imaginative variation, 16 & n.11, 24, 35, 37, 44, 49, 112, 127.
innocent, 93, 95.
intentionality, 57 & n.1, 58, 98, 102, 103, 116.

James, W., 1–2, 18–33, 34, 47, 50, 54, 98.
Johnson, 17.
Jones, Jim, 9.

Kant, 84n.2, 85n.3, 87, 88, 93, 94, 95, 96, 97, 100, 108, 109, 110, 111, 113, 114, 115, 116, 122, 123.
Khomeini, Ayatollah, 9.

Lebenswelt, 76.
limit, 87, 90, 94, 97, 108, 109, 111, 116, 117.

Marx, 118.
Masters, 17.
Merleau-Ponty, 102, 105.
mechanism, 83.
metaphor, 112, 117.

131

morality, 51, 52.
mythic, 11 & n.5, 95, 112, 123.

naturalism, 28, 33, 45, 54.
Nietzsche, 118.
noetic, 46.
noumenon, 90, 108, 111, 116–117, 119.

ontic, 5, 43n.7, 56, 59, 64, 88–91, 92, 100, 103, 104, 105, 106, 115, 119, 125.
ontological, 6, 43n.7, 56, 58, 59 & n.2, 63, 64, 65, 66, 86, 88–91, 94, 103, 104, 105, 124, 125, 126.

passional, 45, 52, 121.
Paul the Apostle, 36, 38 & ff, 42.
phenomenology, 4, 8, 13, 14, 15, 17, 19, 23 & n.26, 24, 25, 33, 34, 37n.3, 42, 45, 53, 56, 57, 60, 68, 71, 72, 73, 76, 79, 81, 83, 91, 98, 100, 101, 107, 116, 121, 126, 127, 128.
phenomenon, 90, 108, 111, 116–117, 119.
philosophical anthropology, 87, 91.
practical, 50, 55.
prephilosophical, 7–18, 63.
prereflective, 7–18, 63.
presuppositions, 3, 4, 5, 7, 12, 17, 18, 19, 33, 56, 59, 60, 63, 64, 65, 66, 69, 70, 71, 72, 79, 81, 101, 105, 127.
primal reality, 26.
psychology, 9, 11.

reduction, 12n.7, 14 & n.9, 16, 18, 127.

reductionism, 83.
regenerated, 93.
regulative idea, 93.
religious qualities, 27, 29.
Ricoeur, 84n.2, 85n.3, 87, 88, 91–98, 107, 108–128.

Sacred, 4, 5, 54, 73–77, 78, 81, 90, 91, 106, 109, 115, 117, 118, 120, 121.
Sartre, 74, 82, 85, 86, 91, 98, 99, 100, 101, 107.
scientism, 14n.8.
secularism, 64, 68, 70, 71, 75n.12.
Skinner, 17.
sociology, 9, 10, 11n.5.
speculative, 2, 26, 69, 112, 128.
Spiegelberg, 19n.13.
supernatural, 27, 28.
symbol, 87, 90, 95, 112, 113, 117.

Teresa of Avila, 47–49.
theism, 5, 8, 12, 28, 29, 36, 54, 59, 60, 73, 74, 76, 120, 121, 127.
theoretical, 51, 55.
"to the thing itself," 13, 15, 18.
total, 90, 107.
Tracy, D., 8n.2, 72, 74, 76–79.
transcendence, 8, 42, 43n.7, 57 & n.1, 69, 86, 91, 94 & n.22, 98, 99, 100, 101, 102–103, 105, 125.
transcendent, 42, 43n.7, 99, 100, 101.

ultimacy, 3, esp. 10n.4, 41 & n.6, 42, 44n.8, 45, 46, 53, 54, 55, 60, 62, 69.

volitional, 45, 52, 121.

"will to believe," 69.